GOTHIC HUDSON VALLEY

Haunted Legends and Ghostly Sightings

Angela Artuso

FONTHILL

Fonthill Media Limited
Fonthill Media LLC
www.fonthillmedia.com
office@fonthillmedia.com

First published 2024

ISBN 978-1-62545-149-1

Typeset in Mrs Eaves XL Serif Narrow
Printed and bound in England

All images were taken by the author unless otherwise noted.

CONTENTS

Acknowledgments

To my wonderful husband, Bill, thank you for your endless love, support, patience, and assistance with all the traveling, the research, and all the interviews during this entire process. Without you, this book would never have been possible, and I am forever grateful.

To my family and friends, thank you for keeping me focused with all your support and positivity.

To my dear friend and mentor, Sam Baltrusis, a special thank you for all your guidance and encouragement. Thank you for Ghost Writers & Spirit Squad and for all the wonderful newfound loving and supportive friends I've made because of it.

Thank you to everyone mentioned in this book for sharing your story!

Introduction

Welcome to the world of ghostly apparitions, eerie sounds, and unexplainable phenomena. Whether you believe in the paranormal or not, there will always be countless ghost stories passed down through generations. These tales often originate from specific locations that are said to be haunted. Whether you are a seasoned paranormal investigator, explorer, researcher, or simply curious about the paranormal, this book will provide you with some of the most popular haunted locations in the lower Hudson Valley of New York.

How does one go about researching and visiting haunted locations? Is it simply a matter of finding the most well-known locations or is there more to it than that? Researching and visiting haunted places can be a very time-consuming task. Before visiting any location, doing as much research as possible is always best. Research includes land history, property history, family history, and the history of the people associated with the property. Many times, records are lost due to fires, demolition of property, or just poor record keeping. There will be times during the research process when you will hit nothing but dead ends. Sometimes, just a simple search in the right location can bring you to long-lost family names and events.

There are many things you need to keep in mind while researching. Names are spelled differently in different time periods. Names given to properties can change to the names of their new property owners. There's a lot of work involved in research that people don't realize until they start doing it. And who knows, you may even uncover some answers to questions that have long been buried. The research process will require scrutiny of historical records, firsthand accounts, and possibly interviews with locals. Online resources like local history websites and paranormal investigation forums can also provide valuable insights. Please note while the thrill of encountering the supernatural can be exciting, it's important to remember to respect these locations and their storied pasts. Many locations will not welcome intrusive behavior, and it's crucial to comply with any rules or regulations that are in place. Two significant rules of the paranormal are always to be respectful and never trespass. One aspect of researching haunted locations is understanding the legends and the stories that are associated with them. It's important to distinguish between fact and fiction, as many popular ghost stories may have been exaggerated or fabricated over time.

Let's dive into what exactly constitutes a haunted location. Is it just an old, abandoned house, or can any place be considered haunted? The truth is, there is no definitive answer. Any location can have a haunting associated with it.

To truly understand the allure of haunted locations, it is essential to delve into their history. Many of these places have a rich and often dark past that contributes to their reputation as being haunted. One of the biggest questions in the paranormal world is why some locations are haunted, and others aren't. That's a tough question to answer. In researching paranormal activity over the years, activity can sometimes be linked to emotion. Locations that have experienced extreme emotional events over the years seem more active than those without. Some locations are associated with tragic events such as murders, suicides, or natural disasters. Others may have a connection to famous figures or historical events. Whatever the case may be, these stories and events add to the mystery and intrigue of these places. These are not just abandoned buildings or tourist attractions—they are places that hold immense significance to the spirits who reside there. So always remember to show respect and treat these locations with care.

Emotions ranging from extreme happiness to extreme devastation can leave a lasting energy imprint on a location. Someone who lived on a specific piece of property that brought them great joy while they were living there may come back to visit that location in their afterlife, perhaps to check in on loved ones they might think are still there, or they could have been a caretaker of a place that they loved so much and feel that they need to come back to help and continue their role as caretaker and/or help the new owners. Locations with tremendous despair or loss of life, such as the Gettysburg battlefield, suicide, and the tragic loss of a loved one, can hold tremendous emotional energy that is transferred over the years. Although none of us truly know the answer, this seems to be the case with many locations.

Furthermore, the history of a haunted location can also provide valuable insight into its potential paranormal activity. Researching past experiences and occurrences at a specific location can help explain any reported hauntings and possibly even identify specific entities or spirits that are said to inhabit the area. Researching the history and layout of a haunted location can help you navigate and identify key areas where paranormal activity is said to occur. This can also provide context for any experiences you may have during your visit. Additionally, understanding the cultural and societal context of a location can also shed light on the beliefs and superstitions surrounding it. This knowledge can help to contextualize any experiences or phenomena encountered during investigations.

So why do people seek out these spine-chilling places? Some are driven by curiosity, while others believe that visiting a haunted location can help them confront certain fears they may carry. For some, it's to help find answers to so many unanswered questions. For others, it's to try and understand why the haunting is there in the first place and try to help bring comfort to the families and lost souls.

Many of these locations will fall into two main types of hauntings. One is an intelligent haunting in which the spirits will communicate with you. They will respond to questions you ask, and you'll be able to hear their responses on recorders and video recordings. You might even physically see a full-bodied apparition trying to communicate with you using hand gestures or pointing out a location. The other type of haunting is known as residual haunting, which is pretty much a haunting that replays itself repeatedly as if it were a video recording being played over and over again. An example of this type of haunting may be someone witnessing an apparition walking through a particular area at the same time each day or night, over and over again. It's a repetitive action that is usually in the same location and occurs at the same time. Residual hauntings don't communicate or interact with anyone.

As you explore haunted locations, you may begin to feel more connected to the energies and spirits that inhabit them. This can be a fascinating and enlightening experience, but it's important to always prioritize your safety and well-being. When visiting haunted locations, safety should be your top priority. Pay attention to any unusual occurrences or sensations during your visit, such as inexplicable noises, sudden cold drafts, or the feeling of being watched. Make note of these experiences and document them for future reference.

After your visit, share your findings with others. Whether it be through written accounts, photographs, or recordings, your insights could contribute to the ongoing research and documentation of haunted locations.

Paranormal research and investigating potentially haunted locations require an open mind and a willingness to believe in things beyond our understanding. With careful planning, respect, and an open mind, you may just uncover the mysteries that lie within these hauntingly beautiful places. Always remember to approach these locations with caution and reverence, as they hold a special place in our history and culture. Visiting haunted locations is not just about seeking thrills or proof of the afterlife. It's also about connecting with history, culture, and the human experience. These places often hold a wealth of knowledge and stories that can teach us about our past and present. So, whether you're a skeptic or a believer, there is something to be gained from exploring haunted locations. You may walk away with a newfound appreciation for the unknown.

While the allure of haunted locations may be strong, taking necessary safety precautions when visiting them is important. This includes researching any potential dangers or hazards associated with the location and taking appropriate measures to protect yourself. It's also important to respect the rules and regulations set in place by the owners or caretakers of the location. This not only ensures your safety but also helps preserve the integrity and history of these places for future visitors.

As a researcher, it's important to approach haunted locations with respect, sensitivity, and responsibility. This means refraining from any disrespectful or harmful activities, such as vandalism or provoking spirits. Provoking during an investigation can cause huge ramifications for the families still living on the property. If you provoke to get a rise out of the spirits and force them to communicate, you leave the family to face the consequences once the investigation is over. Conducting a responsible investigation also involves proper research and documentation of the location's history and reported hauntings. This helps provide a deeper understanding of the location and its potential paranormal activity.

Haunted locations often attract a lot of attention, which can have both positive and negative effects on local communities. On the one hand, it can bring in tourism and boost the economy. On the other hand, it can also disrupt the everyday lives of those living in these communities. It's important to be mindful and respectful of the local community when visiting locations. This includes being considerate of noise levels, following any designated parking or visiting hours, and supporting local businesses during your stay.

Whether you're a believer or skeptic, there's no denying the power of belief when it comes to haunted locations. Our perceptions and beliefs can greatly influence our experiences at these places. It's important to approach investigations with an open mind and avoid letting personal biases or preconceived notions sway your findings. Keeping a neutral mindset allows for more objective observations and conclusions.

The paranormal is a controversial topic, with many debates surrounding its ethics. Some argue that it's disrespectful to disturb or attempt to communicate with spirits, while others believe it's important for understanding the afterlife. As a researcher, it's important to consider the potential consequences of your actions and decisions during investigations. This includes respecting the privacy of any spirits or entities you may encounter and obtaining permission from property owners before conducting investigations.

Exploring haunted locations can be exciting, but it's important to prioritize safety above all else. Always follow designated paths and rules when visiting these places, and never trespass on private property without permission. It's also important to have a plan in place for any potential emergencies or unexpected events. Furthermore, it's crucial to approach investigations with caution and respect. Some spirits may be benevolent, while others may be malevolent. It's important to remain mindful of your surroundings and the potential risks involved in paranormal investigation.

I've spent over two decades researching and visiting haunted locations. It has become a passion and labor of love. Helping others try to understand their experiences has been very fulfilling over the years. I've been an active member of the TAPS Family as well as a longstanding member of the management team. TAPS, short for The Atlantic Paranormal Society, is the team of investigators featured on the TV shows *Ghost Hunters* and *Ghost Nation*. As more and more locations opened up about their ghostly inhabitants and their need for help, investigations flourished, and my involvement, personally, as well as with my team, deepened.

During the research and exploration process for this book, it became evident that some sites, while claiming to be haunted, denied access to anyone seeking information about ghost stories, spooky legends, and anything paranormal. I incurred this issue from several locations, and some were quite curt and rude about it even though their gift shops were filled with books about ghost stories and advertisements for ghost walks. This could have been chalked up to a representative's personal feelings about the paranormal and not that of the actual location itself. Whatever the case may be, these locations have been excluded from this book.

If you find yourself near any of these locations, feel free to explore them. Many are very kind and welcoming establishments that are eager to share their stories, while others carry folklore and ghostly legends for you to ponder. Haunted histories for many locations are often posted on their websites for enthusiasts to enjoy.

Remember to always approach with respect, never trespass, and always remember that ghosts were once people too.

Happy Hauntings!

Bannerman's Castle on Bannerman's Island (Pollepel Island), Beacon, New York

Bannerman's Castle was erected in 1901 by Francis Bannerman, VI, who was a Scottish immigrant who wanted to create a residence that looked just like an old Scottish castle. The castle was built on Pollepel Island, which was its original name. During the American Revolution around 1779, the island had a blockade of iron spikes set at water level which would destroy and sink British ships. When the island was purchased by Bannerman, a canal was formed that became the entrance. The island was used for storing military equipment; when the war ended, it stored leftover ammunition.

Francis Bannerman designed and drew all the plans for the castle and outer buildings, but it remained incomplete after he passed away in 1918. The castle endured frequent lightning strikes due to its numerous flag poles. It also survived a raid by the U.S. Navy during WWI, and a large explosion in 1920, causing major destruction to half of the castle. Some felt that the explosion was caused by lightning, while others felt it was caused by evil spirits. Years later, in 1950, there was another explosion on the island caused by a ship called *The Pollepel* that crashed into it during a storm. The explosion caused even more damage to the castle. After this event, the island became known as Bannerman's Island. The small island's official name was Pollepel Island. According to legend, there was a young girl named Polly Pell who fell in the icy river. She was rescued, married her rescuer, and the island was named after her.

Bad luck continued to hover over the castle and the island. A major transportation ferry to the island sunk, putting an abrupt halt on all visitors and occupants. This, in turn, caused the castle and island to be uninhabited for quite some time. During that time, a fire erupted, causing extreme damage to the interior of the castle.

Native American legend believes that the island is cursed with evil spirits which are responsible for all that has happened on the island. The Indians had always believed the island to be haunted and felt that the evil spirits would come out at night to cause havoc and destruction.

The history of the island goes way back, even before the 1600s, when the Dutch came looking to use it for safety from the Indians. The Dutch believed there were evil goblins, led by the evil Heer of Dunderberg, who were responsible for causing

Bannerman's Castle [*Phreddy Cox CC-BY-SA-4.0*]

severe storms that were treacherous for sailors and claimed tremendous loss of life. In the eighteenth century, a ship called the *Flying Dutchman* was overcome by a severe storm and sank right off Pollepel Island, killing everyone on board. For years following, there have been numerous claims made by fishermen and sailors who say they are able to hear the voices of the dead ghost crew and captain.

Could it be the old Indian legend continuing or is it just a series of bad luck? The island has been associated with numerous legends and ghostly sightings over the years. Some say that the island is possessed by evil spirits, while others believe that goblins control the water and wind surrounding the island. To this day, the island is said to have many strange occurrences. There are claims of a phantom horse being heard galloping across the drawbridge, but there were never any horses present on Bannerman's Island. A strange whistling sound is also heard throughout the island, but its source cannot be located. There are also stories about ghostly apparitions appearing on the island.

It's important to note that many of these paranormal claims are largely based on local folklore and personal experiences and may not be scientifically verifiable. To learn more about the island and its ghostly claims, you can visit HauntedHistoryTrail.org in addition to its website, BannermanCastle.org, which both contain a great deal of history pertaining to the island and castle. The condition of the island and Bannerman's Castle is so treacherous that no one is allowed on the island. The only way to visit is by taking the tour boat that sails past the island. You can see the remains of the castle from the boat. Boat tours and details are listed on their website.

Legends of Haunted Buckout Road, White Plains, New York

The scary urban legends that surround Buckout Road are terrifying. Just imagine driving down this road and needing to worry about running into a serial killer, a bunch of cannibal albinos, and a batch of executed witches.

In the quiet town of White Plains, New York, lies a winding stretch of asphalt known as Buckout Road. Steeped in local legend and whispered tales of the paranormal, Buckout Road has earned a reputation as one of the most haunted places in the region. Many of the stories associated with Buckout Road have been chilling.

Buckout Road got its name from the Buckhout family, who were very prominent figures in the early days of White Plains. The letter H in the Buckhout family name was eventually omitted, and you will see that some of the legends include it, and some don't. The road is spelled without the "h." With deep roots in the community, their homestead on Buckout Road became the epicenter of countless ghost tales and unexplained phenomena. As the stories go, the spirits of the Buckhout family are said to linger, tied to their forever home.

One of the most enduring legends involves Mary Buckhout, a tragic figure whose life took a dark turn. According to local lore, Mary was a young woman who met a tragic end, hanging herself from a tree on the family property. Some say it was heartbreak that led her to take her own life, while others attribute her untimely demise to a more mysterious cause. The ghostly apparition of Mary Buckout is said to wander the grounds of Buckout Road, particularly near the infamous tree where she met her end. Witnesses claim to have seen her apparition dressed in nineteenth-century attire. Some even report hearing whispers or the rustle of leaves, as if Mary's spirit is trying to communicate from beyond the veil.

Mary is not the only member of the Buckhout family believed to haunt the area. John Buckhout, her husband, is said to roam the property as well. The circumstances surrounding John's death are shrouded in mystery, adding another layer of intrigue to the already chilling tales of Buckout Road. Some versions of the story suggest foul play, while others hint at something more sinister causing his death.

Visitors to Buckout Road have reported strange occurrences ranging from inexplicable cold spots and shadowy figures to disembodied voices and ghostly apparitions. The legends surrounding the Buckhout family have transformed the road into a magnet for thrill-seekers and paranormal enthusiasts. Local authorities and historians, however, often dismiss the tales as mere folklore, attributing the ghostly sightings to overactive imaginations and the power of suggestion.

The Curse of Wapeto's Gravesite

Nestled within the dense woods along the infamous Buckout Road in White Plains, New York, lies a mysterious and foreboding gravesite believed to be cursed by ancient forces. The burial ground, known as Wapeto's Gravesite, is said to be the epicenter of paranormal occurrences, while other legends of the area speak of Pathungo's fiery curse that haunts the land.

The legend of Wapeto's Gravesite dates back centuries, intertwining with the rich tapestry of local folklore. According to the stories passed down through generations, Wapeto was a Native American chief who met a tragic end under mysterious circumstances. Some versions of the legend suggest betrayal by his own tribe, while others allude to the meddling of ghostly entities seeking retribution.

The gravesite itself is shrouded in an air of eerie mystery. Local lore tells of inexplicable occurrences surrounding the area such as whispers heard in the wind, strange lights flickering in the night, as well as the ghostly apparition of Wapeto himself. Those who have ventured into the woods near Buckout Road report an unsettling feeling of being watched, as if the spirits of the past are guarding their sacred resting place.

The curse associated with Wapeto's Gravesite is said to bring misfortune to those who dare to disturb the sanctity of the burial ground. Tales abound of ill-fated individuals who, drawn by curiosity or disbelief, sought to uncover the secrets hidden within the woods. Some claim to have experienced a series of unexplained events, from persistent bad luck to unsettling encounters with spectral figures, as if the curse reaches out to punish those who defy its ancient power.

Pathungo's Fiery Wrath

Adjacent to Wapeto's cursed resting place is the legend of Pathungo. Pathungo is said to be a mysterious figure with ties to the occult and is said to have placed a curse upon the land, unleashing a fiery wrath that manifests in strange phenomena and unexplained occurrences. The curse is said to linger like a spectral flame, scorching the earth and leaving an indelible mark on all who cross its path. Witnesses claim to have seen ghostly flames dancing among the trees, whispers carried by the wind, and a strange aura that permeates the area. Some attribute the strange occurrences to the vengeful spirit of Pathungo, while others insist that these are just tall tales and nothing more.

The Mysterious White Deer of Buckout Road

Nestled within the woods surrounding Buckout Road lies a legend that has captivated the imagination of the Siwanoy, the indigenous people of the region. This ancient community, deeply connected to the natural world, embarks on an annual quest each May, seeking the mysterious white deer that are said to appear in the area during the full moon.

The Siwanoy have a rich history of worshipping nature and all its creatures. According to the legend, as the full moon shines upon the landscape, a pristine white deer will emerge from the shadows, moving gracefully through the moonlit forest. It is said that encountering this otherworldly creature will bring blessings and a profound connection to the spiritual realm. The deer is believed to embody the spirit of the land, a guardian of the woods that keeps a natural balance. In Siwanoy tradition, the annual search for the white deer is not merely a quest for a rare sighting but a spiritual journey, a means of communing with the sacred energies that inhabit the realm between the seen and the unseen.

As May approaches, the Siwanoy prepare their traditional dress and honor the traditions passed down to them for generations in preparation for the quest. When the full moon arrives, the Siwanoy set out on their journey through the ancient woods looking for the white deer. The quest is not solely about the physical sighting of the white deer; it is about the spiritual journey itself and the acknowledgment of the delicate balance that exists between the human and natural worlds. The Siwanoy believe that those who approach the quest with pure hearts and open minds may receive the blessing of the white deer, fostering a deeper understanding of life.

The legend of the mysterious white deer on Buckout Road lives on, carried forward by the Siwanoy as a testament to the enduring power of ancient traditions and the timeless enchantment of the natural world.

The Disappearance of John Foster Buckhout and Charlotte Buckhout

In the quiet town of White Plains, New York, the historic Foster-Buckout Road Cemetery stands on Buckout Road as a somber testament to the passage of time and the legacy of families long gone, as well as the site for something very disturbing which took place in 1977.

The cemetery itself is rather small with over fifty burials. Out of all those burials, there is only one headstone that remains, which is the headstone of John Foster Buckhout and his wife, Charlotte. John was the brother of Mary Buckhout. All the other headstones were stolen from the cemetery. Oddly, in 1977, their bodies were dug up and removed. Locals claimed that the bodies were seen propped up as scarecrows on Baldwin Farm. The police never found who did the graveyard raid. They suspected it could have been carried out by a cult of some sort.

No one will ever know why John and Charlotte Buckhout were targeted. Their headstone remains as a chilling reminder of what occurred there in 1977.

The Red Cannibal Albino House

On the outskirts of Buckout Road lies a house that carries a horrific legend for anyone who dares to cross its path. According to legend, a young couple experienced car trouble on a stormy night in front of a small red house on Buckout Road many decades ago. The boyfriend exited the vehicle to assess the situation. Moments later, while inside the car, the girlfriend heard three thumps on the car's roof. In horror, she left the vehicle and saw her boyfriend's feet dangling inches above the car, his body hanging from a tree. The couple is then executed and devoured by a family of cannibal albinos.

Variations of this tale have circulated for generations. While the details may slightly change, the main thing people remember is that if you pull up in front of this particular house and honk your car horn three times, then a clan of cannibal albinos supposedly appear and attack. Some versions of the story suggest that these supposed cannibals lurk in the shadows waiting for someone to come by.

There have been some who claim to have seen strange figures in the windows. Others have reported hearing strange and eerie sounds. We will never really know the true story of the small red house on Buckout Road as it has been torn down. Even though it is no longer there, the legend remains.

The Witches of Buckout Road

Legend has it that three women who lived on Buckout Road were accused of being witches and were condemned and executed by the community. The ghostly spirits of these three women are said to roam the area, possibly in search of retribution for the injustice they suffered. Locals speak of ghostly apparitions seen dancing at night. Some claim to have heard faint whispers as if the witches are trying to communicate with them.

At one point, there were three X's marked on Buckout Road. These mysterious markings, etched into the pavement, are said to symbolize the locations where the accused witches met their untimely end. Each X serves as a spectral marker, a testament to the tragic history that unfolded along the road and as a chilling reminder of the paranormal forces believed to inhabit the area. The legend said that anyone who ran over the X's would have terrible things happen to them. Unfortunately, the road had been repaved and widened; the X's were paved over, and are no longer visible.

The Legend of The Leatherman

In the heart of the woods lining Buckout Road lies an eerie cave, known as Pop's Cave. This landmark was used during the Revolutionary War and was once the dwelling of a very peculiar character known as the Leatherman.

The Leatherman, born possibly as Jules Bourglay around 1839, was a vagabond famous for his handmade leather suit of clothes. He traveled through the Northeastern United States, leaving behind an enduring legend that still captivates people today.

His story is one of mystery and intrigue. The Leatherman was not just a man, but a symbol of resilience and solitude. Clad in a 60-pound leather suit, he was an active figure in the nineteenth century, known for his long walks throughout Connecticut and New York. From his first appearance until the end of his life, the Leatherman devoted every day to walking a 365-mile, 34-day-long, clockwise trip through southwestern Connecticut and adjacent sections of lower New York State. The trips took him through Danbury, New Fairfield, Watertown, Middletown, and New Canaan in Connecticut, and into Westchester, New York, back to Danbury and again to New Fairfield. He would complete this journey every 34 days, regardless of the weather.

The Leatherman was a man of few words, rarely communicating with the locals he encountered on his travels. Yet, his presence was felt by all who came across him. His extraordinary attire, combined with his solitary lifestyle, made him a figure of fascination and curiosity. Despite his silent demeanor, he was known to be harmless, often trading small chores for food or shelter.

Grave of the Leatherman in Sparta Cemetery in Ossining, NY.
[*Find A Grave/Jon*]

Pop's Cave, hidden deep in the forests of Buckout Road, was one of his many stops. This secluded cave, rich in historical significance due to its use during the Revolutionary War, provided him with shelter and isolation. It was here that the Leatherman would spend a great deal of his time, away from the world.

The Leatherman died in 1889; his story continues to inspire folklore and urban legends. A headstone was erected when he died that bore the name Jules Bourglay. Shortly after, it was mysteriously removed and replaced with a headstone that just says Leatherman. The reason for this was never stated so we will never really know his true identity. Numerous attempts have been made to decipher the Leatherman's past and understand his unusual lifestyle, but most have only deepened the mystery surrounding him.

The Dark Tale of Isaac Van Wart Buckhout

The quiet village of Tarrytown, nestled in the heart of Westchester County, New York, was forever marked by a chilling event that unfolded on New Year's Day, 1870. It was a day that would see the birth of a notorious murderer, Isaac Van Wart Buckhout, and the tragic demise of his wife and two other innocent souls.

Isaac Van Wart Buckhout was a member of the Buckhout family who was named after another relative, Isaac Van Wart, who was one of the men who helped apprehend Major John André during the Revolutionary War in Tarrytown, New York.

He accused his wife, Anna Louisa, of having an affair with their neighbor, Alfred Rendall. Isaac savagely beat Ann Louisa to death on New Year's Day in 1870. He then killed Alfred Rendall with a shotgun blast to the face. Alfred's son, Charles, was sitting in the Buckhout's living room when he was shot at close range, causing him to be severely disfigured with the loss of his eye.

Isaac was convicted of murder in 1872 and became the last person sentenced to hang in Westchester County. His ghost is said to wander near his unmarked grave, which is believed to be near his wife's grave.

Regardless of whether you believe in these ghostly legends or not, Buckout Road remains a place of fascination and intrigue. Whether you are curious and eager to explore the haunted tales firsthand or just someone in search of a good ghost story, Buckout Road invites you to step into the shadows and decide for yourself.

Today, Buckout Road attracts thrill-seekers and paranormal enthusiasts hoping to catch a glimpse of the paranormal. A movie was even made in 2017, *The Curse of Buckout Road*, inspired by the mysteries and legends held over the years. Whether these legends are based on truth or the product of vivid imaginations, one thing is for sure: Buckout Road has become an interesting location in White Plains.

Henry Hudson's Ghost Ship on The Hudson River

The Hudson River is known for its many ghostly tales, but the most famous one that has been passed down over the years is of the ghostly sighting of the *Half Moon*. The legend of people witnessing ghostly sightings of Henry Hudson's ship, the *Half Moon*, has been told for years and dates back to the days of Governor Peter Stuyvesant, with sightings of a round and bulky ship flying along the river.

It was on the third day of September in the year 1669, that Henry Hudson, alongside his intrepid crew, navigated the *Half Moon* through the winding path of the Hudson River. Their journey was one of ambition and hope, as they sought a novel passage that would lead them to the riches and wonders of the Orient. The ship made its way north until the majestic Catskill Mountains loomed on the horizon, signaling the crew to anchor and pause in their quest. They gathered, weighed their options, and meticulously planned the next leg of their voyage, ready to face whatever adventures lay ahead.

Late one night, Henry Hudson thought he had heard what sounded like singing and music coming from the mountains. Curious as to what was happening, he decided to head out to the mountains and see what he could find. To his amazement, what he found were very small dwarves with unusually long beards singing and dancing. The little gnomes invited Henry and his crew to their party. They filled them all with food and a special magical potion that the gnomes created which had the ability to transform anyone who drank it into looking like a gnome. As the night went on, Henry noticed that his crew members slowly began to change in appearance. Worried about the effect this was having on himself and his crew, he immediately had everyone return to the ship. As everyone sobered up, their appearances began to return to normal.

There have been many claims of sightings reported by numerous witnesses including sailors, residents, and fishermen who have sworn that they had seen an apparition of the ghost ship sailing along the Hudson River. Legend has it that Henry Hudson returns to the Catskill Mountains every twenty years to once again party with the gnomes.

Vintage postcard of Henry Hudson's Half Moon.

Hulda the Witch, Sleepy Hollow, New York

According to local legend, Hulda, who lived in Sleepy Hollow in 1770, was a doctor who was also branded a witch by the local community.

Hulda was an immigrant from Bohemia who resided in a secluded cabin in the woods. Every day, she wandered through the mystical forest, collecting valuable herbs and creating healing potions that she traded with the indigenous Indians. Her compassion knew no bounds; if someone fell ill, she would anonymously leave a thoughtful basket brimming with medicinal herbs and healing potions at their doorstep.

Based purely on her age, widowhood, and unconventional lifestyle, the narrow-minded townsfolk immediately considered her an outcast. Even the minister of the Old Dutch Church quickly declared her a witch and urged the Sleepy Hollow townspeople not to associate with her.

When the Revolutionary War broke out, Hulda wanted desperately to fight and defend the community. Unfortunately, the people of the town did not want to be associated with her in any way due to the fact they felt she was a witch. Unbeknownst to them, Hulda was an excellent marksman and didn't care what the town thought of her. Even though they treated her so badly, Hulda felt the need to serve and protect her community. She ended up killing several British soldiers before she was shot and killed. According to legend, Hulda was killed by the British on Battle Hill, which was also the location of the Headless Horseman Bridge as told in Washington Irving's story, *The Legend of Sleepy Hollow*.

After Hulda's death was reported, the community found themselves confused as to whether she was truly a witch or an actual hero. She died protecting her community which made her a true patriot. Since Hulda was a practicing witch, she was buried in an unmarked grave in the Old Dutch Church Burial Ground in Sleepy Hollow. When her cabin was searched after her death, a Bible was found along with a will that was found tucked inside its pages. The will had stated that all her gold was to be given to the women of husbands who died fighting for freedom.

In 2019, a ceremony was held to honor Hulda with a memorial headstone. The ceremony was conducted by Reverend Jeffrey Gargano, the pastor of the Old Dutch Church of Sleepy Hollow.
The headstone reads as follows:

Hulda of Bohemia.
Died c. 1777.
Herbalist, Healer, Patriot.
Felled by the British while protecting the Militia.
Buried here in gratitude for her sacrifice.

In *The Legend of Sleepy Hollow*, Washington Irving mentions that Sleepy Hollow was bewitched by a high German doctor. There are many who believe he was referring to Hulda.
The legend of Hulda the Witch turned folk hero adds to the folklore and history that surrounds Sleepy Hollow and Tarrytown, making it a place of deep historical interest for all that visit.

Hulda the Witch, headstone located in Old Dutch Burying Ground.

Kidd's Rock,
Tarrytown, New York

Kidd's Rock, situated in Tarrytown, New York, is a massive rock that has an interesting legend attached to it. According to local folklore, Kidd's Rock was a meeting place for Frederick Philipse and the infamous Captain Kidd, who was a notorious pirate in the seventeenth century. Adding to the mystery is the location of Kidd's Rock, which is in Sleepy Hollow at Kingsland Point Park, an area known for its paranormal activity.

Captain Kidd, a Scottish sailor, was tried and executed for piracy in 1701. According to legend, during his voyages, Kidd hid a significant amount of his treasure along the east coast of the United States. One such rumored location is the legendary Kidd's Rock in Tarrytown. This massive rock, hidden amongst the trees, is said to be the marker of Kidd's buried treasure. Treasure hunters have been visiting Tarrytown for centuries in hopes of discovering the hidden treasure. Although the inscription on the rock reads "Kidd 1690," no treasure has ever been found. The historical landmark also served as a strategic point for troops during the American Revolutionary War.

Today, Kidd's Rock remains an integral part of Tarrytown's landscape, ensuring its preservation for future generations. Its association with the notorious pirate, Captain Kidd, combined with local legend and lore make it a fascinating piece of Tarrytown's cultural heritage. Whether you're a history enthusiast, a lover of mysteries, or simply someone looking to explore unique sites, Kidd's Rock offers an engaging and intriguing experience.

1900s postcard of Kidd's Rock.

King Mansion and the Tarrytown House Estate/ Goosefeather, Tarrytown, New York

"Uplands" was the original name of the white-porticoed King Mansion, which is part of the Tarrytown House Estate that has been overlooking the Hudson River since 1840. It was built using granite from the surrounding areas. It is the oldest building in the Tarrytown House Estate and was named after the railroad executive, Thomas M. King, who purchased it in 1900. Thomas M. King was the Vice President of the Baltimore and Ohio Railroad.

In 1895, the home now known as Biddle Mansion was purchased by William R. Harris, who was the founder of the American Tobacco Company. Thomas King's son, Frederick, married the daughter of William Harris, Sybil, and she was referred to as the "queen" of both estates. In 1921, Mary Duke Biddle of the Duke tobacco family, one of America's richest women, purchased the home from the Harris family. She renamed it "Linden Court." She had pink clay imported from France for her indoor tennis court, which is now known as the Fairfield House, and is still covered by the glass roof she had placed over it in 1933. The bowling alley originally on the lower level of Biddle Mansion is now Cellar 49, a casual curated wine cellar.

Sybil and Frederick Harris continued to live in the King House. When Sybil Harris King passed away in 1955, Mary Biddle purchased the King House and combined the estates. Eventually, the property was sold to a nation in Africa called Mali for a brief time to be used for diplomatic retreats.

In 1964, Tarrytown House Estate was purchased by Robert Schwartz, a journalist and once the editor of *Time* magazine. The house attracted many famous upscale names such as Andy Warhol, Charlton Heston, and Jack Lemmon, to name a few. He felt the house would be the perfect place for businessmen to have a place to retreat.

The Tarrytown House Estate encompasses a collection of notable buildings including the stately, castle-like Biddle Mansion, the charming Carriage House, and the quaint Cottage, all spread across an impressive 26-acre landscape. The estate has recently undergone an extensive multi-million-dollar restoration, ensuring that its beauty and integrity will be preserved for future generations to admire and enjoy.

The mansion's haunted history is well documented. Staff and visitors have reported many strange and unexplainable occurrences including sudden cold spots and temperature drops, objects moving on their own, as well as apparitions. One of the apparitions that was reportedly seen was that of Sybil Harris King (daughter of the co-founder of the American tobacco company, Benjamin Newtown Duke, who died on the second floor of the mansion back in 1955). Sybil was the wife of Frederick King, whose father was Thomas M. King, owner of the King House Mansion and vice president of the Baltimore & Ohio Railroad. An apparition in white, who is believed to be Sybil, has been witnessed walking through the halls on the second floor of the King House. She lingers near room 293, where she is said to have been staying at the time of her passing. Legend states that the spirit of Sybil Harris King likes to play with electronic devices. A guest had once reported that when he woke up, he saw that the date on his phone was changed to 1865. Another guest staying at the mansion stated that his Pandora kept playing the same song, over and over again.

When you enter King Mansion, there is a bar nestled in on the left as you first walk in. Straight ahead is Goosefeather, where Chef Dale Talde, seen on the Food Network TV shows *Top Chef* and *Chopped*, puts a twist on traditional Cantonese cuisine. Not only will you be treated to elegant cuisine, but you'll also have a unique surprise waiting for you at the end of your meal. Your dining tab comes to you presented inside an old, worn, hardcovered book.

One couple's dining experience took a very strange and unexpected turn. They enjoyed their dining experience at Goosefeather so much that they decided to keep the book as a token keepsake of their extraordinary visit. As they ventured back home, their GPS system seemed possessed, relentlessly rerouting them back to King Mansion. Frustration grew as they tried repeatedly to reset it, but to no avail. Their minds couldn't help but connect this bizarre phenomenon to the book they had taken. No matter how many times they tried to reset it, their GPS would insist on taking them back to the mansion. Could it be that the book was somehow connected to this inexplicable phenomenon? Driven by curiosity and a sense of guilt, they made the decision to return the book and apologize to the mansion. And just like that, the GPS stopped rerouting them.

Goosefeather is located on the main floor of King Mansion. Enjoy a dining adventure filled with delicious food, elegant surroundings, and a dash of mystery. Just don't take a book home with you!

The haunted history of the Tarrytown House Estate, King Mansion, and Goosefeather is well noted on their website as well as on the internet and various publications.

Above left: Steps leading to the upstairs guest rooms inside King Mansion.

Above right: King Mansion and entrance to Goosefeather dining room.

Right: Goosefeather places your dining tab inside an old hardcovered book at the end of your meal.

1 La Veta Place, Ghost House of Nyack & The Ghostbuster Ruling, Nyack, New York

One of the most interesting cases regarding a haunting is the home located at 1 LaVeta Place which was built in the town of Nyack, New York, in 1890. The Victorian-style home is said to be haunted by a number of friendly spirits and has been known as the "Ghost House of Nyack." The home gained popularity with its resident ghosts during the early 1990s when it was about to be sold, and the buyer refused to move forward with the sale once they found out the home was haunted due to various publications and its reputation. The case led to what is now taught in law school and referred to as the Ghostbuster Ruling.

Apparitions have been seen in the home including a woman in a flowing white gown, a man with a handlebar mustache, and two children. Apparitions of men dressed in Revolutionary/Colonial attire have also been seen. Slamming doors and the sound of footsteps can be heard throughout the home. They have also been awakened by the shaking of their beds. These spirits and many others are all believed to be former residents of the home.

In the 1970s, the former owner, Helen Ackley, wrote about her family's time spent in the home with its ghostly residents in a *Reader's Digest* article called "Our Haunted House on the Hudson" and how she and her family shared their home with all the different, friendly, ghostly spirits.

In 1989, the Ackley family decided to downsize and put the house up for sale. The house was listed with Richard Ellis of Ellis Realty. The home was listed and priced at just under $800,000, attracting potential buyers, Jeffrey and Patricia Stambovsky.

A short time after the down payment was received, Helen Ackley was notified that the Stambovskys no longer wished to proceed with purchasing the house and filed a lawsuit against her for misrepresenting the material condition of the home, referring to the fact that the Ackley's never mentioned the house had ghosts. Jeffrey and Patricia Stambovsky claimed that the ghost stories devalued the property. Initially, the court dismissed the complaint, stating that Helen Ackley did not have to disclose any ghost-related stories to the Stambovskys. The State of New York operates under the Latin legal term "caveat emptor," which simply means "buyer beware," meaning that it is the buyer's responsibility and not the seller's to ask every question and concern they might have before purchasing a property.

The Stambovskys were unsatisfied with that decision and decided to appeal it. In 1991, the appellate division of the New York Supreme Court agreed to hear the case and concluded that whether or not the ghosts were real, the mere fact that the hauntings were reported and publicized affected the value of the house. Therefore, the house was declared haunted "as a matter of law."

Because she had previously published about her home being haunted and ghostly apparitions, Helen Ackley was unable to deny their existence. However, sticking with the "buyer beware" doctrine, the appellate court held that she was not liable for damages. Instead, due to the fact that "haunted" cannot be easily ascertained with a simple house inspection, the appellate court simply rescinded Stambovskys contract and they were no longer required to buy the house. They did, however, forfeit their down payment.

After the Ackley family relocated, the home has had many new owners over the years and has remained quite quiet in terms of ghostly sightings.

Laurel Grove Cemetery, Port Jervis New York

Laurel Grove Cemetery was founded in 1856 by John Conkling, owner of the land, and is a historical landmark located in Port Jervis, New York. The cemetery is the final resting place for over 14,000 people, many prominent figures in history and includes veterans from the Civil War. Laurel Grove was created during a time when cemeteries were not only a final resting place, but a place where the citizens could take long walks or enjoy a quiet carriage ride.

Additionally, visitors can observe the Tri-State Monument, a landmark stone that marks the location where New York, New Jersey, and Pennsylvania all meet. The Tri-States Monument is located underneath the I-84 bridge. It sits in the middle of the Delaware River known as Carpenter's Point, marking the spot where New York, Pennsylvania, and New Jersey meet.

In a book written by John S. Lindsay, *Mormons in The Theater*, there's mention of a beautiful, famous actress by the name of Julia Dean Hayne who was buried in a plain mound that read "The Unmarked Grave of Julia Dean. New York, August 26, 1897." He describes how he went to the cemetery office to see if he could find any records pertaining to her death. He was shocked to discover that she was a famous actress of the American stage who died during childbirth. His book states the following:

The complete record of the Laurel Grove Cemetery reads:
"Name—Julia Dean-Hayne-Cooper.
«Place and time of nativity—Pleasant Valley, Near Poughkeepsie,
N. Y., July 21, 1830.
"Names of parents—Edwin and Julia Dean.
"Age—Thirty-five years.
"Place and date of death—New York City, May 19, 1866.
"Cause of death—Childbirth.
"Second husband's name—James G. Cooper.
«Buried in Lot No. 3, Section B, owned by her father-in-law,
Mathew H. Cooper.

A path through Laurel Grove Cemetery.

A view of just a small section of the many buried in Laurel Grove Cemetery.

Laurel Grove Cemetery Historical Marker at the cemetery entrance.

«Remains of deceased first placed in the Marble Cemetery General
Receiving Vault, Second Street, New York City. Transferred to
Laurel Grove Cemetery, Port Jervis, April 16, 1868.»

At the foot of her grave is the grave of her unnamed infant daughter who also died with her during childbirth.
It was also stated in her record that all her family had passed away years ago and they are all buried together in the old Clove graveyard in Sussex, New Jersey. Years before Julia passed away, her family had acquired this Port Jervis burial plot so she would have a place for her final rest where she spent her childhood days.

The cemetery is said to be the home to several spirits. Ghostly sightings include seeing a lady in red who appears on foggy evenings and is said to be heard crying for her long-lost love. There are also claims of people seeing an apparition of a lady in white gliding among the headstones. The sound of a phantom train has also been heard passing through the graveyard. Visitors have experienced unexplainable cold spots and apparitions throughout different areas of the cemetery.

Major John André,
Tarrytown, New York

John André was born in London, England, on May 2, 1750. By the year 1771, André had enlisted in the British Army and then three years later, went to Canada after being educated at the University of Geneva. In November 1778, the British commander-in-chief, General Henry Clinton, promoted André to major and named him adjutant general. By 1779, he became deputy adjunct general of the British forces. General Clinton knew that taking over West Point would remove the Hudson River from the Colonials and would force Washington's army into New Jersey. This would cut New England off from the rest of the colonies and leave the French army vulnerable to being captured by the British.

In 1779, twenty-nine-year-old Major John André began to secretly correspond with Margaret Shippen, the wife of American General Benedict Arnold. A year later, Arnold was placed in command of West Point.

On September 20, 1780, Major André sailed up the Hudson River aboard the *Vulture* and met with Benedict Arnold at High Tor Mountain located near Haverstraw. They traveled to the home of Joshua Smith, a friend of Mr. and Mrs. Arnold, where the meeting was concluded. The finalized plan was that Sir Henry Clinton and his forces were to attack West Point on September 25 and Benedict Arnold was to surrender the fort. George Washington was supposed to be away during this time and not expected to return until September 27, at which time he would be seized. In return for this, Benedict Arnold was to be commissioned as brigadier-general of the British army and would be paid the amount of $50,000 in gold.

Major General John André found himself stranded on the shore of the Hudson River. He was supposed to be back on board the British ship, *Vulture*, but it had been chased downriver by cannon fire from the Continentals. Since he could not board back upon the *Vulture*, the plan was for Major André to ride back to British lines and he took with him all the necessary essentials needed to move through enemy territory such as a passport and civilian clothing, using the fake name of John Anderson. Major John André stashed all of Benedict Arnold's signed plans and instructions on how to capture West Point in his boot.

Above left: Major John André [*The New York Public Library Digital Collections*]

Above right: Location where American General Arnold and British Major John André plotted to surrender West Point. Located on the shore pathway south of Haverstraw in the historic Dutchtown area. Today this is part of Hook Mountain State Park. [*NYErik, CC BY-SA 4.0*]

André was riding his horse towards Tarrytown in hopes of making it to New York City, which was now occupied by the British. With approximately 20 miles left to go, he suddenly came across three men, one of which was wearing a Hessian coat. Under the shade of a tulip tree, he greeted them and told them he is a British officer. Suspicious, they force André off his horse and began searching him. They then find the papers from Benedict Arnold hidden in his boot. The report of the capture was received by Major Benjamin Tallmadge, Washington's spy chief, and the documents were ordered to be forwarded to Washington. While dining at the Old '76 House, a courier came to Washington with the plans of West Point which was originally called Fort Benedict Arnold. George Washington didn't believe the plan at first but once he saw the handwriting of Benedict Arnold, he knew it was true. He got up from his table and walked towards the fireplace which was in the dining room. On the mantle, there was a watercolor painting of Benedict Arnold. George Washington walked over to the painting and turned it upside down. Three days later, Major André was brought into the old tavern and was held in custody by Major Tallmadge where he remained until his hanging.

The tavern was actually the stone home of Casparus Mabie which still stands today and is known as the Old '76 House. The house was used often during the American Revolutionary War as a meeting place for the patriots. The original watercolor portrait of Benedict Arnold still remains placed upside down in the Old '76 House.

Major André was admired by Washington and by his American captors. They felt Benedict Arnold should have been the one to be put to death and not John

André. Due to partial retaliation for the hanging of Patriot Nathan Hale, who was captured by the British early in his espionage endeavors, he was denied a trial by court-martial, found guilty of espionage, and sentenced to death. If the event with Nathan Hale didn't take place, Major André's life would have been spared.

On October 2, 1780, Major John André was hanged as a spy on the other side of the Hudson River at Tappan. He was only twenty-eight years old. He was hanged between two cedar trees on Brower Farm and was buried at the site of the gallows in a shallow grave marked by a pile of rocks. The men who captured André were later each rewarded with a farm, a large pension, and a silver medal.

In 1821, Major André's remains were exhumed and transferred to London's Westminster Abbey for reburial. His remains were entombed in a sarcophagus bearing the following inscription: "Universally beloved and esteemed by the Army in which he served and lamented even by his foes."

The original gravesite was marked with two cedar trees at the foot and a flowering peach tree at the head. Unfortunately, the roots of the peach tree grew too large and broke the lid off the coffin and encased André's skull. The tree was removed and transplanted to the garden of James Buchanan, consul general to the Queen, in New York City, but it did not survive, and the empty grave was filled with rocks and a tall stake.

Around 1879, a granite monument was erected to commemorate the site which still stands today, forever marking the location where Major John André died and was buried. The monument was placed on the National Register of Historic Places in 2006. A century after his death, another monument was erected in André's honor at the site of his execution. Inscribed on the monument is the following: "He was more unfortunate than criminal, an accomplished man and a gallant officer." The quote is from George Washington.

In the 1800s, years after André's execution, people of the town reported that the sounds of hoofs were heard as if a madly galloping horse was approaching, but neither a horse nor a horseman were ever seen. Some reported that they saw a gray shadowy figure in the area of a nearby swamp that said the word "halt" in the very same tone that a soldier would use followed by the immediate cease of the galloping sounds they were hearing. Oddly, the sounds were never heard past the old tulip tree, which was known as André's Tree, as Major André was captured beneath it.

When Benedict Arnold died in 1801, the news of his passing reached Tarrytown where the older members of the community gathered at the local tavern for a small celebration. The younger members of the community wanted to get permission from the church to ring the church bell, but suddenly, the sky turned dark, and it appeared that a violent storm was approaching. Suddenly, a big, loud crack of thunder was heard that shook the houses, followed by a huge bolt of lightning. Once the storm cleared, the townspeople saw that André's tree was destroyed and splintered by the lightening.

Eyewitnesses all report hearing the sound of his horse galloping. These sounds were reported each year on the anniversary of his famous capture. It would

Above left: "Andre's place of execution, Tappan, N.Y." [*New York Public Library Digital Collections. Accessed December 1, 2023*]

Above right: "André s Capture Monument" [*New York Public Library Digital Collections. Accessed December 1, 2023*]

almost seem as if the spirit of Major John André returns to Tarrytown over and over again to try to complete his ride and succeed in his mission.

> In the centre of the road stood an enormous tulip-tree, which towered like a giant above all the other trees of the neighborhood and formed a kind of landmark. Its limbs were gnarled and fantastic, large enough to form trunks for ordinary trees, twisting down almost to the earth, and rising again into the air. It was connected with the tragical story of the unfortunate André, who had been taken prisoner hard by; and was universally known by the name of Major André's tree.
>
> *The Legend of Sleepy Hollow* by Washington Irving

The old tulip tree that Washington Irving referred to in The Legend of Sleepy Hollow is no longer standing. It reportedly was destroyed by lightning around the same time Benedict Arnold's death was reported in 1801.

You can visit the site of the hanging marked by a large monument. You can also visit and dine in the same dining room where George Washington is said to have received the documents written by Benedict Arnold in the old tavern/home of Casparus Mabie which is now known as the Old '76 House and in that same room is the blue door in which Major André was brought behind and held as prisoner. It has been said that towards the end of each September, the sound of André's horse's hoofs can be heard echoing down the road, coming to a complete stop at the exact spot where Major John André was apprehended.

Mid Orange Correctional Facility, Warwick New York

Hudson Sports Complex is a 36-acre, multi-million-dollar youth soccer training facility owned by famous soccer player, Christian Fuchs, and his wife, Raluca. It's grand opening was in June of 2019. Hudson Sports Complex is also the former site of the old Mid Orange Correctional Facility.

While undergoing renovations for the training facility, staff noticed they were overwhelmed with tremendous amounts of unexplained activity. Shortly after, we received a call from Kirsten Ibe requesting us to come visit. Kirsten showed us every section of the prison and told us about all the strange and bizarre things that they have experienced some of which we actually experienced during our visit. The lights would turn on and off by themselves while the power was shut off. Music would be heard playing throughout the building while there was no power to the PA system. Some of the activity that was witnessed on all floors of the old prison ranged from hair pulling, unexplained voices, slams, bangs, as well as doors locking and opening by themselves. The lights in the watchtower have also been witnessed going on and off by themselves with no one inside or even near the tower.

There is a massive underground tunnel system that runs throughout the grounds of the prison. Whispers have been heard along with pipes clanking. Inside the Catholic chapel on the fourth floor, there is an extreme heaviness felt that can make it difficult to breathe at times.

During the renovation process, architects would come to evaluate but then quickly leave. Employees have quit after only a few days of being hired. There are fifteen buildings that need to be renovated on the entire complex, but no one wants to work there because of the activity taking place. Strange noises and voices can be heard throughout the prison with no identifiable cause.

Activity first started when tours of the old prison began. Approximately one week before the first prison tour, the lights in the guard tower started going on and off right after the main gate was opened. After the second tour was conducted, a figure was seen walking past the window, but no one was there. During the last weekend of tours, two workers found themselves locked in when the two large doors to the auditorium area slammed shut and locked on their own. When a

Above left: Inside the main entrance of the Hudson Sports Complex.

Above right: The prison watchtower.

Above left: Walkway to the entrance of the prison.

Above right: Main entrance view of the Mid Orange Correctional Facility.

coworker came looking for them, she was able to walk into the auditorium, as the doors were no longer locked. When our team, Gotham Paranormal, did our walk-through and investigation, a tremendously loud and disturbing bang was heard which sounded very much like a desk being thrown in our direction when we were having difficulty unlocking the door to exit. There was no one else in the building at the time. This exit door that would not unlock for us was very eerily located near the same doors to the auditorium that had locked in the staff members.

When Christian and Raluca Fuchs purchased the property to build Hudson Sports Complex, most of the complex had been abandoned. None of the buildings were renovated. So much of the complex had been overgrown, and one could easily get lost. The perimeter of the complex is completely locked and secured. The building that had the most activity was the building at the entrance, which was the vocational school for the prison. The auditorium and stage are still there. When it was a school for boys back in the 1920s and 1930s, a backdrop was painted of all the Sesame Street characters which can still be seen on the stage. Many old chalkboards and baseballs are still lying around the auditorium. Since this building served as a vocational center, religious ceremonies were routinely carried out on the fourth floor for various religious practices.

Before it was the Mid Orange Correctional Facility, it was a home for troubled young boys. The State Training School for Boys officially opened on July 1, 1932. There was a farm on the property and chores were given. Until early 1933, when the first cottages were completed, the boys stayed in a wooden bunkhouse (which no longer exists) and in the Manor House, which was built in 1840 on the foundations of a pre-Revolutionary War farmhouse.

Building for the new training school was largely completed by 1934. The main section consisted of housing and program buildings. There were sixteen two-story, L- shaped cottages. The ground floor contained twelve individual rooms on one wing of the L, with the other wing open and holding about twenty bunk beds. Upstairs were apartments for the cottage parents, usually married couples, who acted as supervisors and guides. The parents who supervised the cottage usually worked from 7 am to 9 pm.

Supplemental buildings provided various programs. The largest building actually consisted of several other smaller buildings. These included the vocational building, the chapel which was converted into a mess hall, the power plant, and the laundry area. There is also the academic building which served as the school, and a gymnasium/auditorium building.

There were two additional two-story buildings that were U-shaped and apart from the main group of buildings. These buildings had an arched entryway and were used as a hospital, offices, a reception area with sixteen rooms, a kitchen, and a dining room. The other U-shaped building was used as a quarantine unit with twenty-two cells for isolation.

Above: The mess hall where prisoners would have their meals.

Below left: A hand-painted mural on the wall of the mess hall.

Below right: A hallway with a metal detector in the back.

Another set of buildings were used for farming. They included barns for the cows, chickens, horses, and a milk house. At some point in the 1960s, farming was discontinued, and the area was then used for storage.

The Training School for Boys was up and running for approximately forty-five years. It held 400 to 500 boys, thirteen to nineteen years of age. It housed mostly the thirteen to fifteen-year-olds but many of the older boys that were there lied about their age to avoid prison terms. All the boys in the program were kept busy with their academic and vocational training. The training school for boys operated as a correctional facility for boys until 1976 and held some of the worst young criminals with histories of pimping, gang involvement, theft, and violent crimes.

One of the most notorious young boys on record was Richard Biegenwald. At the young age of nine, he set fire to his father's home and underwent electroshock therapy. During his stay at the facility, he was accused of stealing and inciting others to escape. He was never reformed, and as an adult, became a prolific serial killer who ended up murdering nine people before he was caught.

Shortly after WWI, the facility was created to be a treatment facility for those dealing with drug and alcohol addiction. It later became a boy's correctional facility, then finally, in 1976, it was converted into the Mid-Orange Correctional Facility. The first inmates arrived at the prison on June 29, 1977, and operated as a medium-security prison for men until it closed in 2011.

Hudson Sports Complex continues with its renovations and is now a state-of-the-art soccer training facility owned by soccer star, Christian Fuchs and his wife, Raluca. However, the school building remains untouched and riddled with paranormal activity, likely due to all the residual energy left over from all the years of housing inmates who committed mild to severe crimes and the plethora of emotions that they harbored.

The complex has been featured on television shows such as *Ghost Nation* and has become a hot spot for paranormal investigators and enthusiasts. During the year, paranormal tours and investigations are available for those wishing to try and experience activity. During the Halloween season, the former prison is transformed into a walk-through haunted house that attracts huge crowds of visitors who can't wait to get frightened by what's behind its walls. Activity reported has been that of hair pulling, doors locking and unlocking by themselves, items being thrown, sounds of running, sounds of children laughing, and the sounds of disembodied voices heard on all the floors. Information about tours and ongoing events can be found on their website, www.HudsonSportsComplex.com.

Left: One of the many hallway doors of the prison.

Below left: The visitors' entrance area of the prison is located near the auditorium.

Below right: The auditorium and visitors' area of the prison.

11

Miss Fanny's Party House, Wappinger Falls, New York

Featured on various television shows such as *Haunted Collector* and *My Ghost Story* is the infamous Miss Fanny's Party House.

Stephen Van Wyck was born on June 22, 1850. In 1872, he married Elizabeth Underwood, and they had two children, Robert M. and Charles. Robert was born on January 16, 1896, and later became a bookkeeper for a chair factory. He later married a woman named Louise Luckey and they had one child, a daughter, named Fanny Elizabeth Van Wyck. The farmhouse she lived in originally belonged to her great-grandfather, Cornelius Van Wyck, and once stood on Lake Walton Road and Van Wyck Lane until it burned to the ground sometime in the 1800s, but the date has not been clearly documented. After the fire, the home was rebuilt, and the kitchen that was once part of the original home was put into the new home, which is now Miss Fanny's.

Fanny Van Wyck was born on April 6, 1903, into a well-to-do family of high social standing. In 1923, she married Charles Boos who was equal in the social graces. The home they lived in was built by Fanny's grandfather for her father and then, eventually, it became hers. Fanny and Charles turned their home into a beautiful Victorian-style mansion which is now known as Miss Fanny's Victorian Party House in Wappinger Falls, New York.

Fanny was a remarkably interesting woman who always kept herself busy. In the 1950s, she attended the New York State College for Teachers at New Paltz as a full-time student. She also had a pilot's license and would fly in to attend classes three times a week. She was a teacher at Poughkeepsie Day School, the chairman of the American Red Cross in the Town of East Fishkill, the chairman of the East Fishkill unit of the American Cancer Association, president of the Fishkill Plains Library, treasurer of the Dutchess County Library Association, member of the East Fishkill Recreation Association, recording secretary of the Mid-Hudson Aviation Association, and corresponding secretary of Gallaudet home. She was also an avid world traveler.

She was known for having lavish parties and would often invite friends for dinner and dancing and many barn parties. She was an animal lover.

Fanny Van Wyck was extremely interested in the paranormal. She would invite psychics to come to the house and hold sessions in the library, which she

Above left: Old historical photo of the house as shown on their website. [*missfannys.com*]

Above right: An article posted in the Poughkeepsie Sunday New Yorker about Fanny Boos. [*Poughkeepsie Sunday New Yorker Dec 17, 1988*]

would record. She once traveled to England and attended a ghost hunt. When she returned, she felt as though she had brought home with her the spirit of a young girl. A young child's voice whispering "mommy" has often been heard in the house and captured on EVPs during paranormal investigations. Along with the child ghost, there is evidence of a man shadow figure and a woman who may be Fanny herself protecting her home.

There is also an old, handed-down story of a farming accident that took place back in 1920 when a young girl was apparently using some farming equipment on the property. Her hair accidentally got snagged in the turning gears and she was scalped to death. Her body was later found by the owners. She was never identified, and her name was never given in any of the papers that reported the accident.

Fanny Van Wyck-Boos was the last to live at the home and when she died, the home was willed to the town to be kept open to the public and preserved. Fanny wished her home to be used as a museum and to remain open to the people of the town. Unfortunately, the town auctioned off the entire contents of her home. The home was purchased by Julia Drahos, who has continued running it for over twenty years.

The home was featured on an episode of *Haunted Collector* over ten years ago. An interesting finding was discovered during that episode. Since the homeowner, Julia, loved to collect odd items and antiques, she had in her possession a casket plate which she had displayed on the wall. A casket plate was used to identify the caskets that sat in receiving vaults where they stayed until warmer weather conditions would allow the ground to soften so they could be buried. The coffin plate was engraved with the name Lucy D. Perrin. She died in 1872 at age twenty-eight. Normally, that would be attached to the coffin itself and buried, but for some unknown reason, this plate wasn't. It's quite possible that when she was buried, the elements and time loosened the plate and it eventually detached from the casket. When further research was done, it was discovered that Lucy had died in a fire caused by an unattended candle, and her body was buried in Connecticut. In hopes of clearing out a good deal of any paranormal activity taking place in the home, John Zaffis brought the plate back to her grave in Connecticut and buried it with her. It may have worked for any energy that may have been surrounding that particular item, but the house remains filled with paranormal activity. What made it this unusual was the fact that when Miss Fanny's was rebuilt after the initial tragic fire that took place on the property many years ago, the home was rebuilt using recycled wood that was recovered from another location that had burned down. The fact that Lucy D. Perrin perished in a fire was an eerie coincidence.

Julia and her family have had their fair share of strange and unexplainable experiences. She has seen apparitions, heard footsteps, disembodied voices, the sounds of laughing children, and all the usual occurrences that come with a home inhabited by spirits over the years. The owner has even seen a huge human figure in the headlights of her car. When she went to question him, he disappeared through the siding of the home. Neighbors have had their share of experiences too. Of interest is the fact that Julia and Fanny Van Wyck have so much in common and they both have shared their love for the paranormal. The current owners of Miss Fanny's enjoy sharing their stories and welcome paranormal investigators to come visit the home to experience all the ghostly happenings for themselves. The home is listed on the National Historical Register. Paranormal investigators are welcome to book their investigations at the house and share their experiences along with some true ghostly hospitality.

A photo Lucie D. Perrin, the woman who died in a fire and was connected to the coffin plate that was found. [*missfannys.com*]

12

Old Dutch Reformed Church and Old Dutch Burial Ground, Sleepy Hollow, New York

Adjacent to Sleepy Hollow Cemetery is the Old Dutch Church of Sleepy Hollow, a historic church that was built in 1697 by Frederick Phillips. It's the oldest church in New York state and one of the oldest in the country. The churchyard contains graves dating back to the seventeenth century, including those of early Dutch settlers. Washington Irving's story, *The Legend of Sleepy Hollow*, is set in the vicinity of this church. The Old Dutch Church and its cemetery were designated as a National Historic Landmark in 1961.

The Legend of Sleepy Hollow was brought to life by famed author, Washington Irving. In the story, the schoolmaster, Ichabod Crane, is on his way home after proposing to Katrina. The night is dark, and he is walking alone. Suddenly, the Headless Horseman appears carrying his pumpkin head on horseback, chasing after Ichabod Crane. The Headless Horseman, riding on his black horse, throws his Jack-o-Lantern pumpkin head at him and Ichabod mysteriously disappears, never to be seen or heard from again.

As mentioned in the Tales of the Old Dutch Burial Ground by the Friends of The Old Dutch Church and Burial Ground (odcfriends.org), many of the characters in Washington Irving's tale were inspired by real people during that time period. Three of those people were buried in The Old Dutch Burial Ground located alongside the Old Dutch Church. It is said that the real inspiration for Katrina Van Tassel was Eleanor van Tassel Bush, but the character's name was borrowed from a woman named Catalina Van Tessel. The character of Brom Bones was inspired by Abraham Martling. As for the Headless Horseman, it is said that the body of a Hessian soldier was decapitated by a cannonball in 1776. His body was found and buried by the Van Tassel family in an unmarked clearing area in the Old Dutch Burial Ground in the northeast corner. This unmarked area was also used to bury others non-deserving of headstones.

Eleanor Bush was born Eleanor Van Tassel, a very beautiful Dutch maiden whose father was Revolutionary officer, Jacob Van Tassel. His grave is also in the burial ground. Their family lived on a farm "hard by the banks of the Hudson" which was later purchased by Washington Irving and named "Sunnyside."

Above left: A wall plaque from 1697 at the entrance of the Old Dutch Church.

Above right: Welcome sign inside the Burying Ground at the Old Dutch Church.

Right: Side view of Old Dutch Church Old Dutch and Burying Ground.

Old Dutch Church Burying Ground looking into the connecting Sleepy Hollow Cemetery.

The site is listed on the National Register of Historic Places and is the oldest house of worship in New York. The church remains an active place of worship, and its congregation continues to celebrate its rich history and cultural heritage. It holds religious services on Easter and Christmas Eve, as well as weddings and funerals.

Info pertaining to guided tours of the cemetery can be found online. Self-guided visits are free from April through November.

13

Silvio's Italian Villa, Warwick New York

Silvio's Italian Villa is an exquisite Italian restaurant located in Warwick, New York, that dates back to the eighteenth century. It was first occupied by a Revolutionary War veteran named Levi Ellis. Ellis was born in 1745 and grew up in Warwick, where he enlisted in the Continental Army at the age of thirty-one. He fought alongside George Washington's troops and served for six years until the end of the war. During his time as a soldier, Ellis was known for his bravery and strong leadership skills.

After the war, Ellis returned to Warwick and continued to serve his community. He became a farmer and established a successful business, cultivating apples and producing cider vinegar. Ellis was also known for sharing his wealth with those in need, always striving to help others in the community.

Today, Silvio's Italian Villa stands as a tribute to this remarkable man. The property has been owned by the same family for over fifty years and continues to serve as a beloved restaurant in Warwick. The owners take great pride in preserving the history of the property and honoring Ellis' legacy by serving authentic Italian cuisine while also supporting local farmers and businesses. Visiting Silvio's Italian Villa not only allows guests to indulge in delicious food but also offers a unique opportunity to connect with Warwick's rich history.

In 1920 Harry Vail purchased the property what was then known as Maple Glen Farm. The Vail family continued to own the property until tragedy struck in 1972. Roy Vail's sister was found murdered but no one was ever caught and charged for the murder. Over the years, suspicion began to grow and was cast on Roy who was a famous gunsmith. Ten years later, he committed suicide in the Peach Room of their home.

The home was turned into an Italian restaurant, now known as Silvio's Italian Villa. Guests say that they have seen objects move on their own, doors open and close, and have seen apparitions of a young girl and cat appear and then vanish. The restaurant has been featured in various publications and TV shows such as *Haunted Collector*. Paranormal investigations have captured recorded EVPs (electronic voice phenomenon), glowing orbs, sounds of footsteps, and rapidly

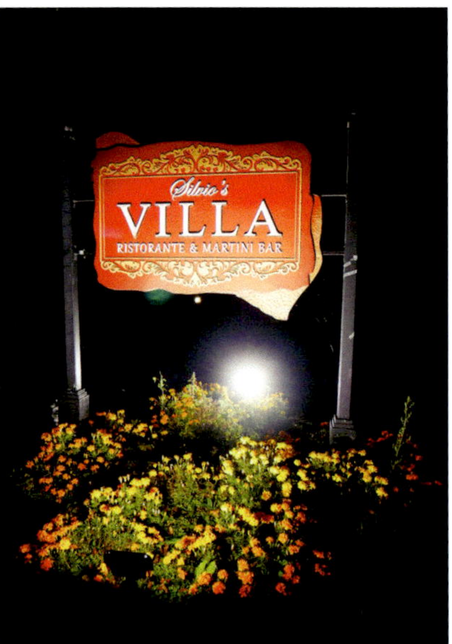

Above left: The sign for Sylvio's Italian Villa

Above right: Sylvio's walkway entrance to the restaurant.

wilting flowers. Staff and guests report a door opening on its own, missing objects, and the apparition of a little girl. Diners at Table 24, seated beneath the site of a tragic suicide, are often treated to a bit of unusual activity with their dinner. Table 24 is the actual site where Roy Vail took his life.

Silvio's Italian Villa, located at 274 NY-94, Warwick, NY, is an establishment that blends history, culture, and cuisine in a unique way. It is not just its history or its food, but the ghost stories that are associated with it. The villa is featured on the Haunted History Trail of New York State and is considered a haunted place by many. These stories add a sense of mystery and adventure to the dining experience at Silvio's Italian Villa.

Above left: Memorial plaque in memory of Roy Vail hangs on the wall near Table 24.

Above right: Table 24, the site where Roy Vail took his life.

Below left: The bar area inside the restaurant.

Below right: Photo of Roy Vail placed on Table 24.

News article from Advertiser Photo News covering the murder of Miss Emily Vail. [*Advertiser Photo News, August 8, 1974*]

14

Sleepy Hollow Cemetery, Sleepy Hollow, New York

Sleepy Hollow Cemetery, located in Sleepy Hollow, New York, was established in 1849 and spans over 90 acres. It's famously known as the final resting place of author Washington Irving, who immortalized the cemetery in his tale, *The Legend of Sleepy Hollow*. Irving's tale of the ghastly Headless Horseman who supposedly haunts this area has become interwoven with the cemetery's identity. Many visitors and locals alike claim to have encountered ghostly sightings, particularly near the grave of the author himself. This strong association with the paranormal has made the cemetery a popular destination for paranormal enthusiasts and those intrigued by its haunted history.

The story of the Headless Horseman is a chilling tale that has its roots in American folklore. It is said that the Horseman was a Hessian soldier during the American Revolutionary War who was decapitated by a cannonball during a fierce battle. According to legend, the horseman was unable to find peace in the afterlife after being separated from his body, and he now haunts the cemetery, riding his spectral horse through the night. Legend has it that he is on an endless search for his missing head, and any unfortunate soul who crosses his path is at risk of losing theirs as he attempts to replace what he has lost.

Over the years, there have been various anecdotal accounts of ghost sightings at the Sleepy Hollow Cemetery. Visitors and locals alike have reported unexplained occurrences, such as sudden chills, strange noises, and fleeting apparitions. These spectral sightings often align with the legends and folklore associated with the cemetery, adding to the mystery and allure of this historic site.

Sleepy Hollow Cemetery is the final resting place for many. Sometimes, it included pets. In 1892, little Leo, the cocker spaniel, died, and his owner, Jessie Gillender, had a coffin specially made for him. She purchased a small burial plot in Sleepy Hollow Cemetery and had the dog buried there. She loved and missed Leo very much and would visit his grave often. She even paid neighborhood children to go with her. A neighboring plot owner was angered over the dog burial and all her visits, so one night, he stole the coffin and left it on a nearby bridge. Karma kicked in and at some point, that evening, he fell off the bridge and broke his leg.

Above left: A plaque inside Sleepy Hollow Cemetery telling of the legend of the Headless Horseman.

Above right: Sleepy Hollow Cemetery

Right: The Headless Horseman bridge marker.

Below left: Sleepy Hollow Cemetery Gate

Below right: The Headless Horseman reconstructed bridge.

MISS GILLENDER'S "DARLING LEO."

A MASONRY VAULT FOR THE COCKER SPANIEL WHICH SHE MOURNS.

WHITE PLAINS, N. Y., Dec. 5.—A curious case came before the Grand Jury here to-day. It was an attempt to indict John O'Keefe and John Tracy of Tarrytown for opening a grave in Sleepy Hollow Cemetery, Tarrytown, and taking therefrom a coffin containing the body of a pet dog.

This dog in its lifetime belonged to Miss Jessie Gillender, who occupied the Kingsland house. She is the daughter of Arthur Gillender, a wealthy tobacco merchant in New-York. The dog, a Cocker spaniel named Leo, died last August, and her grief for it was deep and genuine. She went to a number of undertakers to have a coffin prepared for its interment, but none of them would have anything to do with such a queer proceeding. Finally she got Thomas Kane to undertake the job for $30, and a silver plate, bearing the words "Our Darling Leo," was placed upon the coffin.

The lady then went to the Superintendent of the Sleepy Hollow Cemetery and purchased a plot for $37 near where the gurgling Pocantico River flows on its way to the Hudson, and overlooked by the proud mausoleums of George Lewis, D. Ogden Mills, Gen. Delevan, Manton Marble, and others. The grave of Washington Irving is not far away.

The dog in its coffin was duly buried there and the story is current that she went there almost daily and cried over it and got the children of the vicinity to accompany her, always paying them from 50 cents to $1 when the ceremonies were over. One little Italian used to save up all his tears and wait at the gate for Miss Gillender to come and pay him $1 as a mourner for "our darling Leo."

One night, however, the grave was opened by unknown persons and the coffin and "our darling Leo" carried away. The next morning the coffin and its canine occupant were found near a bridge not far away. O'Keefe has a plot in the cemetery near the one in which the dog was interred, and had objected to the whole proceeding. He was found on the night of the disappearance of the dog's body, near the bridge, having fallen off it and broken a leg, and was helped to the home of William H. Hyland, where he was cared for.

These circumstances led some to believe that he was the ghoul who invaded the cemetery and stole "our darling Leo," and that John Tracy was in some way connected with him. The case was considered by the Grand Jury to-day, but no bill was found against them.

Miss Gillender, upon the recovery of the coffin with its contents intact, had a masonry vault built in the plot, the coffin replaced and sealed up so tightly that nothing short of dynamite can now open it, and therein "our darling Leo" is supposed to be peacefully lying after all his vicissitudes.

Miss Gillender's Darling Leo article as posted in The New York Times. [*The New York Times*, 12-06-1892]

He was caught for his grave robbing and Miss Gillender was able to get the coffin back with little Leo inside. She subsequently had a masonry vault built for Leo and had it sealed so tightly that it could never be opened so that little Leo could rest peacefully.

Buried in the cemetery are several notable figures, which include Washington Irving, the renowned author of *The Legend of Sleepy Hollow* and *Rip Van Winkle*; Andrew Carnegie, industrialist, and philanthropist; Walter Chrysler, the founder of the Chrysler Corporation; Brooke Astor, socialite and philanthropist; Elizabeth Arden, founder of the cosmetics company, Elizabeth Arden; and Leona Helmsley, real estate mogul known as "The Queen of Mean." Also laid to rest here is William Rockefeller, a co-founder of Standard Oil.

Above left: Washington Irving's gravesite.

Above right: The Irving Family plot.

Above left: Andrew Carnegie stone monument at his gravesite.

Above right: William Rockefeller's mausoleum.

Some of the most notable figures buried in the cemetery include:

John Dustin Archbold (1848-1916), a director of the Standard Oil Company

Viola Allen (1869-1948), actress

Elizabeth Arden (1878-1966), businesswoman who built a cosmetics empire

Brooke Astor (1902-2007), philanthropist and socialite

Vincent Astor (1891-1959), philanthropist

Leo Baekeland (1863-1944), the father of plastic; Bakelite is named for him.

Holbrook Blinn (1872-1928), American actor

Henry E. Bliss (1870-1955), devised the Bliss library classification system

Major Edward Bowes (1874-1946), early radio star, host of *Major Bowes' Amateur Hour*

Andrew Carnegie (1835-1919), businessman and philanthropist

Louise Whitfield Carnegie (1857-1946), wife of Andrew Carnegie

Walter Chrysler (1875-1940), businessman, founded the Chrysler Corporation

Francis Pharcellus Church (1839-1906), editor at the *New York Sun* who penned the editorial "Yes, Virginia, there is a Santa Claus"

Kent Cooper (1880-1965), influential head of the Associated Press from 1925 to 1948

Jasper Francis Cropsey (1823-1900), landscape painter and architect

Maud Earl (1864-1943), British-American painter of canines

Parker Feimelly (1891-1988), American actor

Malcolm Webster Ford (1862-1902), champion amateur athlete and journalist; brother of Paul, he took his own life after slaying his brother

Paul Leicester Ford (1865-1902), editor, bibliographer, novelist, and biographer

Samuel Gompers (1850-1924), founder of the American Federation of Labor

Walter S. Gurnee (1805-1903), a mayor of Chicago

Mark Hellinger (1903-1947), primarily known as a journalist of New York theatre; Mark Hellinger Theatre in New York City is named for him; produced The Naked City, a 1948 black-and-white film noir

Harry Helmsley (1909-1997), real estate mogul who built a company that became one of the biggest property holders in the United States, and his wife Leona Helmsley (1920-2007), in a mausoleum with a stained-glass panorama of the Manhattan skyline.

Raymond Mathewson Hood (1881-1934), architect

Washington Irving (1783-1859), author of *The Legend of Sleepy Hollow* and *Rip Van Winkle*

George Jones (1811-1891), one of the founders of the *New York Times*

Ann Lohman (1812-1878) a.k.a. Madame Rested, nineteenth-century purveyor of patent medicine and abortions

Darius Ogden Mills (1825-1910), made a fortune during California's gold rush and expanded his wealth further through New York City real estate

Whitelaw Reid (1837-1912), journalist and editor of the *New York Tribune*, vice presidential candidate with Benjamin Harrison in 1892, defeated by Adlai E. Stevenson I; son-in-law of D. O. Mills

William Rockefeller (1841-1922), New York head of the Standard Oil Company

Edgar Evertson Saltus (1855-1921), American novelist

Francis Saltus Saltus (1849-1889), American decadent poet and bohemian

Carl Schurz (1820-1906), senator, secretary of the interior under Rutherford B. Hayes.

William Boyce Thompson (1869-1930), founder of Newmont Mining and financier

Joseph Urban (1872-1933), architect and theatre set designer

Henry Villard (1835-1900), railroad baron

Oswald Garrison Villard (1872-1949), son of Henry Villard and grandson of William Lloyd Garrison; one of the founders of the National Association for the Advancement of Colored People

Paul Warburg (1868-1932), German-American banker and early advocate of the U. S Federal Reserve system

Worcester Reed Warner (1846-1929), mechanical engineer and manufacturer of telescopes

Thomas J. Watson (1870-1955), transformed a small manufacturer of adding machines into IBM

Hans Zinsser (1878-1940), microbiologist and a prolific author

The cemetery is open for guided tours for those who are interested in getting a closer look and education about the history of the location. Special programs and tour information are noted on their website.

15

Spook Rock and Raven Rock, Tarrytown, New York

While searching the archives and various publications for more information about the legendary Spook Rock, I quickly learned that there are actually several different Spook Rocks scattered around various parts of New York, all with their own story to tell. The Spook Rock that I'm referring to here is the one located in the Rockefeller State Park Preserve in Tarrytown. In this preserve stands another famous rock that has a legend connected to it called Raven Rock.

Back in the 1800s, the elderly folk of Tarrytown, New York, would often tell the story of Spook Rock as it was told to them by their parents and their grandparents. The rock was an ancient landmark long before the legend of Hulda the Witch was even mentioned. According to Indian legend, the rock was an ancient Indian shrine to the medicine men of the Leni Lenapes and the Sachems.

According to legend, a young Indian man was returning from a late-night hunt. He began to see lights moving in the direction of the rock along with musical voices. Curious as to what it could be, he moved closer to the rock and saw a dozen of the most beautiful women he had ever seen holding hands and dancing upon the rock. In the center was a basket, which, according to his lore, was the chosen vessel that celestials would use when visiting from the heavens. They were dancing so lightly that he compared it to a bundle of leaves being lifted by the air, swirling in a circle. As the women were dancing, the young Indian man continued to watch in wonder and amazement at the most beautiful sight he had ever seen.

When they looked up and saw the man watching them, they quickly hurried into the basket, but the most beautiful one of them all stopped and stared at the Indian man. The other women reached out to grab her into the basket as they were all singing and laughing. In an instant, they were all gone, and the Indian man was left standing there completely alone. The young man looked up at the sky and saw a super bright shining star thinking that was probably the home they were returning to.

He kept returning to the rock in hopes of seeing the women and the basket again. It is not entirely known how long this continued and whether it was weeks or months, but the basket eventually returned to the rock, and the women were again seen dancing on the rock. Once again, they suddenly began to disperse, but the young man grabbed the

Above left: Spook Rock [*Melissa Martin CC BY-NC-SA 2.0 DEED*]

Above right: Raven Rock [William Owens "Pocantico Hills 1609-1959"]

most beautiful one of all and took her home with him. The celestial woman became his wife, and they had a child together. Years later, the sound of the women singing was once again heard and his wife could be heard murmuring the same songs as the women. The next night, the young man's wife was missing. He continued to care for the baby the best he could, but the baby just cried and cried, refusing to eat anything it was given, and eventually died. He buried the baby in a grave by the Pocantico River. After mourning for some time, he went hunting but never returned.

In the springtime, several years later, the star wife returned thinking she was only gone for a few hours and not realizing how much time had actually passed. Thinking something was wrong, she searched for her home up and down the Pocantico woods.

To this day, bright sparkling lights have been reported at night in the area of Spook Rock, especially during the springtime. It is said that if you listen closely enough, you can hear the star woman crying out for her baby and her lover. You can find Spook Rock by hiking the Spook Rock Trail in the Rockefeller Preserve.

In this same preserve is another rock named Raven Rock, named after the ravens that circled the forest centuries ago. Legend says the ghostly image of a lady in white can be seen with cries that sound as though the wind is howling. It is said that she got lost in a snowstorm and took shelter under the rock where she died.

Another legend told of Raven Rock is that of an Indian maiden who met her fate at the hands of a jealous lover. She is said to be seen roaming the area lamenting her fate.

The rock isn't easy to get to. It's deep inside the preserve and one has to go up and down steep slopes and winding turns to get to it.

You can hike the trails throughout the preserve and visit both rocks. There are lots of other interesting locations in the preserve as well including the location where Hulda the Witch's old home once stood. Maps and destination guides of Rockefeller State Park Preserve can be downloaded on the website FriendsRock.org.

16

Tarrytown Music Hall, Tarrytown, New York

The Tarrytown Music Hall, nestled in the heart of Tarrytown, New York, stands as a testament to the rich cultural tapestry of the region. Throughout its storied history, this venerable institution has been recognized far and wide for its contributions to the arts. As the oldest theater in Westchester County, it has become a beacon of entertainment, drawing patrons from near and far. The Music Hall recently reached a milestone, celebrating its 138th year anniversary, a remarkable testament to its enduring presence in the community.

Constructed in the year 1885 by the esteemed William Wallace, a famous chocolatier, the theater was envisioned as a palace for the performing arts. Wallace's legacy is embedded in the very foundations of the building, which has served as a grand stage for a myriad of performances. The theater's opulent design and acoustics have made it an ideal venue for a diverse array of cultural events.

Over the years, the Tarrytown Music Hall has played host to a large mix of artistic expressions. The venue is known for featuring a diverse range of acts, including music concerts, comedy shows, and more. From classical to contemporary concerts, comedy shows, children's performances, and recitals, as well as theatrical productions, the theater has been a hub for creativity. It has welcomed a parade of talent across its stage, with actors, musicians, and performers of all genres gracing the audience with their craft. The hall has also been a gathering place for various cultural events that celebrate the arts, providing a sense of community and shared experience among those who walk through its doors. Tarrytown Music Hall's longevity and success are a reflection of its unwavering commitment to the arts and the community it serves.

Stepping into the grand music hall, one could almost hear the echoes of its illustrious past, a past that was carefully crafted by none other than Robert Goldblatt, the original owner of this magnificent establishment. Goldblatt was also the founder of the Washington Irving Trust Company. In the year 1885, the hall was filled with a variety of entertainment and became well known for its vaudeville performances. Acts at the theater included horse shows, flower shows from mansions and greenhouses, the suffragettes, May West, Teddy Roosevelt, Woodrow Wilson, Charlie Chaplin, and so much more. It has consistently continued to host numerous artists over the years.

Above left: The lobby of Tarrytown Music Hall. *[Michael Artuso]*

Above right: The ghost light on the stage always stays lit.

When there are no performances taking place, you will find a lit ghost light on the theater stage, so the theater will never without light. The ghost light is considered a beacon in the darkness of an empty theater. It is a symbol of respect and a time-honored tradition that has been passed down through generations of performers and theater staff. This solitary light serves as a guide, an ever-burning flame that ensures the spirits of those who have graced the stage with their presence can always find their way back.

There are several interpretations of the ghost light, each steeped in the rich history and lore of the theater. Some say it's a practical measure, a way to ward off mischievous spirits or to keep the theater's own ghosts contented and at peace. Others view it as a safety measure, ensuring that those who walk the stage after the audience has departed do not stumble in the darkness.

One of the most common understandings of the ghost light is the idea that we leave a light on as a symbol of continuity and remembrance. It's a beacon for the past, present, and future of the theater. It's very similar to a lighthouse that shines across the ocean of time, guiding the souls of actors, playwrights, directors, and stagehands back to the heart of their theatrical home. The ghost light embodies this phrase "to always find your light" in the most literal and figurative sense. It's the perpetual light that ensures no matter how much time has passed, no matter how far one has roamed, there will always be a way back to the stage, back to the light, back to the essence of the theater itself.

The music hall has had its share of people passing through over the years, many of whom have come and gone. It is felt that many of the spirits that passed on return to the music hall from time to time to return to a place they loved. Whether it be a past worker at the theater, a past performer, or perhaps just a theatergoer, the presence of various spirits has been experienced by many at the music hall.

The second-floor dressing room is a hotbed area of strange activity for the staff. The old production manager said it was haunted. He always heard voices and had strange experiences backstage. One night he was locking up and heard the house manager singing. The next day he told her she had a nice voice, but she was already long gone, and no one was there. A piano has also been heard playing. It has been reported by staff that unexplainable voices have been heard in response to staff making performance calls of "call 5" and "places."

Paranormal investigations conducted by Gotham Paranormal Research Society and by staff and visitors have found that the dressing room areas seem to be two hot spots for paranormal activity. In particular, the upstairs dressing room has quite a few unexplainable events that have taken place in that area. There's an ongoing feeling of uneasiness causing people to feel very uncomfortable to the point where they don't want to stay. A medium once refused to stay in that area. Equipment has been known to go on and off as well as tip over from no known cause. After a performance, the production director was on stage putting things away along with another staff member when they heard men talking from the second-floor dressing room. They also heard what sounded like someone singing warm-ups as if they were preparing for a performance. When they went to look, no one was there. While researching, it was found that a Republican presidential candidate, Henry Dodge Estabrook, came to the theater to see a movie but died in the theater. The exact location of his death is unclear as some reports state he died in his seat and others say he passed while being carried out to the lobby.

When the theater is closed up for the evening and everything is shut down, staff have reported seeing a light turn back on in the dressing room from the parking lot after the building had been locked for the evening and everyone had gone home. One night, one of the workers tried to pull back one of the dressing room curtains. While he was pulling, he felt a strong resistance and tugging on the curtain as if someone was tugging back.

The regular lower-level dressing room is usually reserved for roadies, warm-up bands, tour managers, etc. This is the area that is usually set for the artist's dinner, and it's decorated nicely. The dressing rooms are multifunctional for all different types of events.

There is a crossover on the stage that allows performers to exit the stage, go through the basement, and come up to the stage on the other side. The basement stores music stands and xylophones, and anyone who goes down there has feelings of being watched. People feel like they're hearing things and feel as though someone is standing right next to them, but no one is there.

A few years back, there was a production of Oliver which was performed by a children's theater. A photographer came during the day to take photos of the children. While she had them positioned on stage and ready to take the photos,

Above: View of the theater from the stage.

Right: An article that was found indicating that Republican presidential candidate Henry Dodge Estabrook died in the theater. [*The Sun, 12-23-1917*]

Below: The lower-level dressing room where singing and voices have been heard.

H.D. ESTABROOK DIES IN A MOVIE THEATRE

Prominent Lawyer and Republican Politician Stricken in Tarrytown Music Hall.

WON FAME AS AN ORATOR

Entered Race for President in 1916 in the Nebraska Primaries.

Henry Dodge Estabrook, formerly solicitor-general of the Western Union Telegraph Company, a lawyer of national reputation and an aspirant for the Republican nomination for President in the last campaign, died suddenly at 8:45 o'clock last night while attending a motion picture show in the Music Hall at Tarrytown. He was seen to swoon in his seat and when carried out into the lobby Dr. Owen Igoe, who was in the theatre, found that he had died of heart disease superinduced by acute indigestion.

Mr. Estabrook was in apparent good health Friday when he appeared as counsel for the people of Tarrytown before Justice Tompkins and argued for two hours against paving Broadway in his home town with a make of pavement on which the village trustees had voted approval but to which his clients were opposed.

Although he was 63 years old he had seemed to be in specially good health for the last several years during which he had been very active in public affairs. In recent months, in fact since the last political campaign was ended, he had devoted most of his time to his private practice as a member of the law firm of Noble, Estabrook & McHarg, whose offices are at 115 Broadway, Manhattan.

Was Reared in Nebraska.

Mr. Estabrook was born in Alden, N. Y., October 23, 1854, the son of Experience and Caroline Augusta Estabrook. His father at one time was the Attorney-General of the Territory of Nebraska. Through his paternal grandmother he was a descendant of the Puritan John Alden.

Mr. Estabrook came into national prominence when, as a "favorite son" of Nebraska, he announced his candidacy for the Republican nomination for President at a dinner given in his honor, August 21, 1915, in San Francisco, by Frederick W. Adams, treasurer of the American Bar Association. He carried his candidacy through seriously, establishing large headquarters adjoining his law firm's offices and carrying on a national propaganda. He announced his withdrawal, however, when the national Republican convention met in Chicago in May, 1916.

Mr. Estabrook had for many years previous to that been prominent in Republican politics. It was asserted by his political backers during his campaign for the nomination that he was responsible for the election of President McKinley. He was also referred to as the man who rounded up the Southern delegates for Theodore Roosevelt at the Republican National Convention in 1912. For his political help it was known that President McKinley once offered him an ambassadorship, which Mr. Estabrook declined. Indeed, he refused many political offers and never held an elective office except that of regent of the Nebraska State University.

Prominent as Orator.

Besides his ability as a lawyer Mr. Estabrook rose to prominence through his oratory. In the last few years he spoke many times at large affairs on preparedness. When he was seeking the Presidential nomination his slogan was "Protection, Prosperity and Preparedness." He was a bitter assailant of President Wilson and Mr. Bryan because of their then pacifist views, and he consistently followed Roosevelt, except when the former President took his stand on the referendum and recall, to which Mr. Estabrook was determinedly opposed.

Mr. Estabrook was frequently called upon to speak and act as toastmaster at banquets given in honor of famous persons and at special celebrations and ceremonies. He delivered the address at the unveiling of the Thomas Nast painting "The Surrender of Appomattox" and at the unveiling of the famous Lincoln statue in Lincoln Park, Chicago.

Mr. Estabrook's early education was received in the public schools of Omaha, Neb., where his father went in 1855. His father, formerly District Attorney-General of Wisconsin and a member of the Constitutional Convention of that State, was appointed United States Attorney for Nebraska on the passage of the Kansas-Nebraska act. The son was named for Henry Dodge, a former Governor of Wisconsin and United States Senator from that State.

Began as Newspaper Carrier.

While attending the public school in Omaha Henry Dodge Estabrook carried newspapers for the Omaha *Tribune*. He later became a reporter for that paper and while in the work took up the study of law. He received his higher education at the Washington University in St. Louis, from which he was graduated with a bachelor of laws degree in 1875. In 1896 he was admitted to the bar and after practising a while in Omaha removed to Chicago, where he became a member of the law firm of Lowden, Estabrook & Davis.

A sister, who died in 1897, was the wife of Robert C. Clowry, later president of the Western Union Telegraph Company. For a number of years Mr. Estabrook was local attorney for the Western Union in Omaha and Chicago and in 1902 was appointed solicitor in New York city.

During the many years of service he appeared in many notable litigations and in his private practice several of his cases established important practice. As a member of the American Bar Association he was made chairman of the committee on judicial administration and remedial procedure. He held this office at the time of his death and also was a director of the New York County Lawyers Association.

Mr. Estabrook was a member of the New York State Bar Association, the American Bar Association, an honorary member of the Canadian Bar Association, also of the Grant Club of Des Moines, Ia.; a member of the Lawyers, Union League, Lotos, Metropolitan, Ardsley, Sleepy Hollow and Republican clubs of New York and the Automobile Club of America.

He married October 23, 1879, Clara, the daughter of Oliver C. Campbell of Omaha, Neb. Their daughter, Blanche Duel, is the wife of Karl G. Roebling of

she kept seeing a child hanging around in the background that wasn't part of the production, making shadows over the group photo. When she asked for someone to help escort the child off the stage, everyone turned around only to find that there was no child there. The child was only able to be seen in the viewfinder.

From the stage, some claim to have seen people in the projection room when no one was there. They also have seen people sitting in the balcony from time to time. There was also a sighting of what appeared to be a man standing on one of the ladders fixing the lights on the side of the balcony. Again, no one was there. During a paranormal investigation, Gotham Paranormal Research Society heard the sounds of a piano playing and a xylophone coming from the basement. Also noted were the sandbags and pulley systems on the stage swinging back and forth with no reasonable explanation. During one of their investigations, while standing in front of the stage and talking with staff, a man entered the theater and came walking towards everyone. When everyone quickly glanced and asked each other who that was, everyone turned to find the man was completely gone. It was felt that the apparition could have possibly been one of the older staff members who was well-loved and passed away several years ago.

Occasionally, one will hear whistling throughout the theater. One of the staff members who passed away used to whistle while he worked. The whistling could also be from staff members who worked at the music hall over the years but are now long gone. In the days of yore, when sailors would dock their ships at port, they often sought out additional employment to fill the time between their sea-bound adventures. These seafarers, with their well-honed skills, found that they were particularly well-suited to the bustling world of the theater. They were highly skilled at tying a myriad of complex knots which made them the perfect candidates for managing the intricate overhead pulley systems that were essential to the theatrical productions of the time. The sailors would handle the ropes and pulleys, ensuring that the various set pieces and curtains glided smoothly across the stage. Of interest, when it came to communication, they brought a unique aspect of their nautical life to the theater. Instead of raising their voices, shouting, and yelling, they would whistle to each other. It was a method that sailors used while at sea to signal important actions like lowering or raising the mast.

The sandbag pully system that is located on the side of the stage.

The language of whistles became an invaluable tool backstage in theater. In an era long before modern communication devices such as headsets and walkie-talkies, these whistling codes allowed the stagehands to coordinate complex scene changes and cue actions without disrupting the performance with shouted instructions. The skills that these sailors had mastered on the high seas translated into the art of stagecraft, making them indispensable members of the theater community.

In the 1930s, there was a transition over to more cinema and gradually away from vaudeville performances. In the 1930s, the balcony windows were covered to prevent light from coming in for the movie theater. Tinted glass can still be seen from the stage, but it is covered. There is a projection booth at the top. Before renovations were done, the balcony used to be shorter and lower. Behind the balcony, there is office space which at one time used to be residences. The seats in the balcony are from the 1930s, and if you look closely, you will see holes under them. These holes were used to hold a shelf where gentlemen would place their hats. The balcony seats have under-balcony lighting. People claim to see people sitting in the balcony section, but no one is there. Singing has also been heard in the balcony. The balcony has lighting racks with a type of pully system used to lower lights to change the bulbs. Shortly after 1904, the music hall was purchased by Moses and Mary Newman, who replaced all the gas chandeliers with electric ones.

The projection room sits above the balcony. One night when the projectionists had left for the night, the stage director saw the light on in the projection room and someone walking right through the light. Once again, no one was there. People often see people walking in the projection room, especially from the orchestra area and stage. A feeling of extreme heaviness is often felt in this area.

There are some residences located upstairs as well as the offices. The balcony is original to the theater, as are the box office windows. There is studio space upstairs along with a theater arts program for kids. VIP parties are held in the private area upstairs, and a special entrance is used. Just about everything is original. There is also a member lounge for members of the music hall to come before a show.

The theater was in danger of being demolished in the late 1970s but was saved by new owners, Berthold F. Ringeisen, Ph.D., a founding board member of "The Friends of The Mozartina" and his wife, Helen. They put up their life savings to save the beloved theater. The music hall was officially saved from the wrecking ball on February 14, 1980, Valentine's Day. Since the music hall was in such an array, structural renovations were done, leaky ceilings were fixed, and a new foundation was placed.

Tarrytown Music Hall has hosted a variety of performers across different genres over the years. Approximately 80,000 people come through the doors each year and over 200 shows are performed each year. Its haunted reputation isn't just a recent development. It is part of the Haunted History Trail of New York State and offers guided ghost tours of the music hall. Whether you're a skeptic or a believer, the Tarrytown Music Hall promises an unforgettable experience filled with history, culture, and perhaps some unexplainable happenings during your visit.

Left: A view from the balcony lighting rack area inside Tarrytown Music Hall.

Below left: The projector booth above the balcony where shadowy images have been seen walking back and forth

Below right: Inside the projector room where whistling has been heard.

17

The Ghost of Sybil Ludington, Carmel, New York

In Carmel, New York, Sybil Ludington was an intriguing figure in American history and often referred to as the female Paul Revere. At only sixteen years old, she played an extraordinary role in the Revolutionary War.

Sybil Ludington was born on April 5, 1761, in Fredericksburg, New York, to Colonel Henry Ludington and his wife, Abigail. She was the eldest of twelve siblings and was given many responsibilities that one would expect to be part of a very prominent family. The Ludingtons were deeply involved in their community, and Colonel Ludington, in particular, played a pivotal role in local military affairs.

Colonel Henry Ludington was a veteran of the French and Indian War. He held a significant rank in the local militia and was entrusted with the defense of his community. The Ludington home was situated in what is now known as Ludingtonville.

In the years leading up to the American Revolution, the Ludingtons were acutely aware of the growing tensions between the colonies and the British. Even though Sybil Ludington was sixteen years old, she witnessed and understood her community's need and strong desire for independence, which was enhanced by her father's very strong military service. As time went on, she became more aware of the gravity of the situation they were in. As hostilities escalated, discussions were held about the fate of the colonies, and the Ludington family, along with many other families, grappled with the decision to support the revolutionary cause.

The British Army, along with loyalists, attacked and burned Danbury, Connecticut. During the raid, a messenger was sent to the home of Colonel Henry Ludington asking for help. The militia had a duty to rally the troops and prepare to defend themselves against the enemy, but they needed someone to urgently notify the militia what was happening. On a stormy night in the spring of 1777, Sybil mounted her horse and rode 40 miles to rally local militia troops against the British attack on Danbury. She rode tirelessly, knocking on doors and rallying the local militia to respond to the imminent threat. Sybil's journey covered treacherous terrain, taking her through rain-soaked woods, muddy roads, and unfamiliar territories. The troops weren't able to save Danbury, but they were able to stop the British advance and force them back to their boats on Long Island Sound. This became part of the Battle of Ridgefield on April 27, 1777.

Sybil Ludington's midnight ride may not have earned the same historical spotlight as Paul Revere's ride, but it carried great significance during the Revolutionary War. Her courageous journey through the night played a key role in mobilizing local militia units, ensuring that reinforcements reached Danbury in time to engage the British forces. The successful defense of Danbury not only dealt a blow to the British in the region but also boosted the morale of the Continental Army and its supporters. Sybil Ludington's actions demonstrated that the fight for independence was not confined to battlefields but extended to the courage and commitment of individuals, even those as young as sixteen.

Sybil Ludington married Edmond Ogden on February 14, 1784. They had one son, Henry, named after Sybil's father. The Ludington-Ogden family settled in Catskill, New York, where they led a relatively quiet life. She lived to the age of seventy-seven and was buried in the same cemetery as her father.

Sybil Ludington did not receive recognition for her fearless ride until the late nineteenth century, when a statue depicting her and her horse during that fateful midnight ride was erected in her honor in Carmel, New York. The inscription on the statue commemorates her role in the defense of Danbury and emphasizes the importance of her contributions to the cause of American independence. The bronze statue was sculpted by Anna Hyatt Huntington, and it depicts Sybil Ludington riding on horseback, screaming, and waving the stick that she used to knock on doors and anyone who got in her way. The statue was dedicated on June 3, 1961. In addition to the statue, various historical markers and plaques have been dedicated to Sybil Ludington, ensuring her story is not forgotten. Local commemorations, including annual rides in her honor, have become traditions in the regions where she made her historic journey, placing Sybil Ludington alongside the many other American heroes and heroines.

The supposed route that Sybil took for her infamous ride can be seen today by the historical markers created to celebrate the 150th anniversary of the American Revolution. Her ride has been commemorated with a statue that graces the shores of Carmel's Lake Gleneida.

Carmel and the surrounding areas are heavily filled with burial grounds for both Native Americans and settlers, making the place a prime hot spot for paranormal activity along with the many deaths during the Revolutionary War on that same soil. Legend states that some have heard the sound of Sybil and her horse riding through the streets, reenacting her famous ride.

Sybil Ludington's grave. Of note is the different spelling of her name on her headstone. [*Michael Herrick, November 10, 2009/Historical Marker Database*]

18

The Bull's Head Inn, Cobleskill, New York

The Bull's Head Inn was built in 1802. It sits on the same site as three previous structures that date back to 1752 when George Ferster built one of the very first buildings in Cobleskill, New York. On May 30, 1778, during the American Revolution in the Battle of Cobleskill, that home was completely burned to the ground by Indians, Tories, and the British. Nearly all the settlements were burned and many of the retreating patriots were scalped and murdered.

After that building was burned down, two others were built. They were also burned down and then rebuilt in 1781. It is said that residents perished in one or more of the fires, including a girl in an upstairs bedroom who was too terrified to run and died in the blaze.

The current Bull's Head Inn was built in 1802 and served as an inn and tavern. It was purchased as a private residence by Charles Courter who died in the building on January 1, 1879.

The last private residents of the Bull's Head Inn were Mr. John Steacy and Mrs. Grace Steacy. It is said that Mrs. Steacy was a member of the Woman's Christian Temperance Union. She loathed alcohol and drinking while John Steacy was quite the opposite. When they passed away, the estate was sold to Monte Allen who was the mayor of Cobleskill.

The Inn changed hands many times over the years. It was once a town hall, a courthouse and meeting hall, and a masonic temple. It was an inn, then a private residence, then back to an inn again in the 1960s. Monte Allen reopened the Bull's Head Inn as a restaurant in 1966. He also added a bar to the home which was placed where Mrs. Steacy's bedroom used to be.

There have been numerous claims of apparitions being seen by guests and staff. One in particular is said to be the spirit of Mrs. Steacy wearing a white gown and moving around the staircase and its upper and lower landings. There have been numerous reports of food, napkins, plates, etc. being thrown across the room. People hear doors slam shut as well as faucets turning on by themselves.

There's also a story of a guest who stayed at the Bull's Head Inn with his family who fell ill one day and stayed in his room while his parents went sightseeing.

He took a nap in the rocking chair of the room and had a horrible nightmare of being locked in a room in a cabin surrounded by flames. No matter how hard he tried to get out of the room, he couldn't open the door and couldn't find a way out. He suddenly woke up to a tugging on his arm which he thought was his sister waking him. When he looked again, he saw a young girl in period clothing. It was the young girl that had perished in the fire on the site of the Bull's Head Inn years ago.

The Bull's Head Inn is a historical landmark and a favorite location for paranormal enthusiasts to visit. As advertised on their site, they book paranormal investigations, haunted tours, and haunted dining.

Bull's Head Inn [*Facebook/BullsHeadInnCobleskill*]

19

Burn Brae Mansion, Glen Spey, New York

The Burn Brae Mansion was built by Charles and Margaret Mackenzie Elkin in 1908 and became one of the family's last three surviving mansions. Margaret was the daughter of George Ross Mackenzie, the third president of the Singer Sewing Machine Company. George Ross Mackenzie died in March of 1892. Upon George's death in 1892, his children built additional mansions in Glen Spey. George's estate was estimated to be valued at $3.5 million. His daughter, Margaret, and her husband, Charles Elkin, built Burn Brae Mansion as the last family mansion and one of only three still surviving.

It is believed that the house was designed by prominent architect Henry Janeway Hardenbergh, who worked on a number of projects for Singer executives. Hardenbergh is most known for designing several of the most famous buildings in New York, such as the original Waldorf-Astoria Hotel, the world-famous Plaza Hotel on Fifth Avenue, and the Dakota apartments on Manhattan's Upper West Side.

Charles Elkin was an engineer and inventor. He had a patent for the Elkin Hose Clamp and for the mouthpieces on pipes and cigars. Charles owned a spring water bottling business located behind the mansion near the woods. He was an accomplished organist. Margaret continued her father's tradition of donating to many charities, and she enjoyed throwing lavish parties.

Margaret and Charles had a daughter, Elsey Elkin, who died at the age of four years old on April 22, 1893. Their son, Charles Jr., died at age thirty-four on February 27, 1919. Sadly, their grandchild, Levi, was born then quickly died shortly after in 1940.

Burn Brae Mansion has had five owners since the Elkins, and over the years it has served as a boarding house, a speakeasy, a tearoom during prohibition, a restaurant in the 1950s, and a bed and breakfast. Even though the mansion has changed hands several times after the Elkins had owned it, it seems as though the original owners had never left.

The current owners, Mike and Pat Fraysse, bought the house in 1993. When they purchased the property, it had been operating as an apartment house. Even though the house was in a severe run-down condition, they decided to purchase it and begin renovating it and bringing it back to life. They currently operate the house with their daughter, Susan, and son-in-law, Andy, as a bed and breakfast, which also includes a twelve-room motel where the former horse stables once stood. Once the mansion opened up as a bed and breakfast, all kinds of strange activity started to be reported.

Burn Brae Mansion has a reputation for being haunted. Visitors and guests over the years claim that the attic is haunted and is the central location responsible for any of its guests' ghostly experiences. Previous owners, guests, and visitors have reported strange and unexplained occurrences. These include apparitions, footsteps heard in the hallway, the sound of babies crying, the sound of furniture moving, disembodied voices, doors opening and slamming, voices of children, balls bouncing, apparitions of a man in overalls, and one in turn-of-the-century clothing. Visitors have reported hearing the sound of an organ playing as well as the sounds of animals, but neither were present. A good portion of the activity seems to be coming from the attic. Some have heard a baby crying in the middle of the night when there were no babies present in the mansion. A family member has seen a white light traveling down the stairs with an outlined image of a woman in a white nightgown appearing shortly after.

The Fraysee's daughter, Susan, and her husband, Andy, stayed in the Mackenzie room of the house. They ran a recorder during the night to see if they could pick anything up. They closed the door and went to bed. At around 3 o'clock in the morning, they both woke to the door slamming shut. Not sure what to make of it, they played back the recorder to see if it captured anything. At approximately ten minutes before the door slammed shut, you can hear the door being opened on the recorder. Whatever it was, entered their room and stayed for about a good ten minutes and then left, slamming the door. Guests who stay in the Mackenzie Room have reported that they have seen the apparition of a man sitting on the steps that lead to the bathroom.

When they were having work done to repair some leaks in the roof, workers found what appeared to be a sealed off room when they pulled back the insulation. In the room was a crib, children's toys, a picture on the wall, and a doll. The 10 x 8 sized room was completely walled off and sealed off with sheet rock.

When the mansion had tenants a short while back, two were noted to have died in the house. They were an elderly couple named the Hapijs who were both in their 90s. It has been reported by guests that their ghostly images have been seen in the front yard playing chess. Renters may have moved out over the years, but it appears that Burn Brae has its resident spirits who live there permanently, rent-free.

Guests who visit the mansion will find a collection of Singer sewing machines. They are also encouraged to explore the "attic of curiosities," which holds an enormous collection of antique dolls. Guests will find dolls scattered throughout the entire house. Many of them were found in the house when the Fraysse's bought the mansion, many are family-owned, and many have been sent to the mansion over the years. The attic is full of dolls, toys, collectibles, antique furniture, old clothes, and lots of other interesting items. There is also a collection of old horse saddles, one of which was owned by John Wayne.

Multiple people claim to have witnessed a sad lady in white sitting on the steps in the servant's hallway. Other claims include balls bouncing in the attic, electronic devices not working properly, quickly draining batteries, and doors opening and closing by themselves. Some people hear animals in the house, but none are present, and many have heard the voices of children.

In 2015, Jason Hawes and the team from the show *Ghost Hunters* investigated the property. They returned again in 2020, at which time activity seemed to intensify.

Burn Brae Mansion appears to have a peaceful history. There is no record of any murders or violent activity ever taking place. The nearby Glen Spey Cemetery is the final resting place for several members of the Elkin family as well as the two elderly tenants, the Hapijs, who passed away in their apartment.

Burn Brae Mansion advertises their events year-round and has been on several paranormal TV shows. They welcome guests and paranormal investigators to come visit and seek out their resident spirits.

Burn Brae Mansion

20

The Curse of the Bronze Lady, Sleepy Hollow, New York

According to local lore of Sleepy Hollow Cemetery, the Bronze Lady monument is an imposing statue of a woman seated in grief. The Bronze Lady is a twice-life-size bronze statue of a seated woman, located across from the grave of Civil War General Samuel Thomas. Thomas was a noted steel manufacturer, railroad executive, and mine owner. The statue was sculpted by Andrew O'Connor, Jr., and was created at the request of Thomas' widow. The statue was created in 1903 and is said to be one of the most haunted places in the cemetery. The widow is said to have been filled with such sorrow that she visited the statue daily, rain or shine, until her own passing. Over time, the Bronze Lady took on a life of its own, with locals claiming to see the statue weeping or moving on its own, further cementing its status as a captivating piece of local folklore.

The model for this imposing statue was Jesse Phoebe Brown, mistress of the sculptor, O'Connor. Her likeness can be seen in several other sculptures by O'Connor, but none have garnered the supernatural attention that the Bronze Lady has attracted. Unlike the infamous Headless Horseman, the Bronze Lady doesn't roam the grounds causing mayhem. Instead, she sits quietly, forever waiting, casting an eerie presence over the cemetery. It's this stillness and silence that have led to whispers of a curse and have drawn locals and tourists to her. The stories say that the Bronze Lady comes alive at night and that her eyes glow with an unnatural light. It's said that anyone who dares disrespect her by sitting on her lap, especially under the moonlight, is likely to encounter a string of unfortunate events, or worse, a tragic end. Some say a curse will be placed upon anyone who touches her face or they might see bloody tears. If anyone looks into the keyhole of the mausoleum, they might see a vision of a ghost. Stories of eerie happenings, including visions of the lady weeping or the feeling of an unseen hand pushing trespassers away, have added to the statue's haunted reputation. However, the origins of this curse remain a mystery.

Gothic Hudson Valley

Above left: The Bronze Lady statue.

Above right: Close-up of the face of The Bronze Lady statue.

The Bronze Lady statue faces the mausoleum of General Samuel Thomas.

The Enslin House, Troy, New York

The Enslin Mansion in Troy, New York, was built in 1890. The home was purchased by Frederick Anthony Feyl in 1919 after he and his wife came to New York from Bavaria. The home has been passed down and family-owned for generations. The Bell family had owned the Enslin House for six generations.

In the 1920s, the home was a well-known supper club. One of its famous guests included frequent visits by the notorious gangster and bootlegger, "Legs" Diamond, who would come by to eat dinner in the dining room.

There are numerous spirits that roam the Enslin home. Many of the spirits are members of the Bell family. There is also a spirit of a woman named Shirley, who was living in the home at one time and was found dead in the basement. It was said that she was pushed down the stairs, but no one was ever able to find out who could have possibly pushed her to her death. People have reported being pushed and shoved in the home.

Michele Bell was the owner of the property for quite some time and posted the home for sale in 2021 through her real estate company. Over the years, she has had numerous personal experiences, including capturing the voice of her teenage son, who passed away from cancer. The home is listed as a "Haunted House in Upstate New York" and can be rented by those who wish to have their own haunted experience.

The Pine Bush UFO Museum, Pine Bush, New York

Pine Bush, a small hamlet nestled in the Hudson Valley of New York, has been noted as being a hotbed of Unidentified Flying Object (UFO) sightings and paranormal activities. Since the early 1980s, there have been reports of strange lights and objects in the sky, often described as discs or triangular-shaped crafts exhibiting extraordinary maneuverability and speed.

Some of the most compelling stories come from individuals who have lived in Pine Bush for decades. They recount experiences of seeing glowing orbs, triangle-shaped craft, bright lights that change color, and objects that move in ways that defy conventional aviation technology.

Despite the skeptics, UFO enthusiasts, researchers, and curious visitors have been coming to Pine Bush for years. Many of them come with their cameras, hoping to catch a glimpse of a passing UFO. The town's night sky has become an unofficial observatory for those seeking an encounter of the third kind.

Pine Bush's UFO history is also linked to the nearby military base, Stewart Air Force Base. Some attribute the sightings to experimental military aircraft, while others insist they are clearly extraterrestrial in origin. The Pine Bush UFO Museum provides a captivating journey into this enduring mystery.

The Pine Bush UFO Museum also serves as a gathering place for those interested in UFO phenomena, playing host to several events, including the annual Pine Bush UFO Fair. This event features guest speakers who are experts in the field, vendors selling UFO-themed merchandise, and a parade that embodies the spirit of Pine Bush's unique culture. The annual Pine Bush UFO Fair's special guest list includes Travis Walton, Thom Reed, and Kathleen Marden, who share their experiences regarding UFO abductions.

While there, you can stop by the nearby Cup and Saucer Diner, a UFO-themed diner with a massive menu that can satisfy anything you wish for.

The sightings, the stories, and the Pine Bush Museum have made Pine Bush one of the most intriguing destinations for those seeking encounters with the unknown.

The Shanley Hotel, Napanoch, New York

The Shanley Hotel resides in the town of Napanoch, New York. It is in the foothills of the Shawangunk Mountains in beautiful Ulster County in Upstate New York. The hotel has been a historic bed and breakfast for well over 100 years. The Shanley's doors are always revolving, welcoming new guests who come to visit and explore its history, paranormal enthusiasts from all over to experience its paranormal activity, and of course, its well-known guests who never left. Even in the spirit world, ghostly guests are forever finding this hotel and checking in. The hotel is under new ownership, and the new owners are very warm and welcoming, providing tours and making reservations for all who wish to stay at the infamous hotel.

The history of The Shanley Hotel begins in 1845 when a man named Thomas Ritch erected the Ritch's Hotel on Main Street. The setting seemed perfect, being a popular vacation spot for people escaping city life as well as being located right by the railroad, which would attract travelers looking for a place to spend the night. Ritch had created an elite Gentleman's Club for his male guests, which allowed them use of the upstairs bordello.

Six years later, in 1851, Thomas Ritch sold the hotel to Mr. Hungerford, and the property was then renamed Hungerford's Hotel. Mr. Hungerford continued making sure the bordello remained active.

The hotel continued to change ownership over the next thirty-six years, until 1887 when it was taken over by Adolph Wagner. Unfortunately, eight years later, on March 18, 1895, ambers from a nearby fire fell onto the hotel, tragically burning it down to the ground. Adolph Wagner quickly rebuilt and got the hotel back up and running by November of the same year.

In 1906, the hotel was, once again, up for sale. On October 1, 1906, the hotel was purchased by James Shanley and renamed The Shanley Hotel. Mr. Shanley added a bowling alley to the hotel, a billiard room, and a barber shop to the building. James Shanley met and married Beatrice Rowley at the hotel on April 26, 1910, and honeymooned in Washington, D.C.

The Shanley's loved to entertain guests and hold lavish parties and events. They were well known for their card and domino tournaments. Beatrice Shanley would

Above left: The Shanley Hotel

Above right: This side view of The Shanley faces the area where little Rosie died in the well, directly across the street. This image was taken from the well.

often hold high tea parties and social events. Famous guests at the hotel included Thomas Edison as well as Eleanor Roosevelt, who was the best friend of Beatrice Shanley. James and Beatrice were so close to the Roosevelts that they were even invited to attend the Inaugural Ball for President Franklin D. Roosevelt.

The Shanley's, unfortunately, had three children, all of whom had died at very young ages. Kathleen lived only 6six months, James lived only four-and-a-half months, and William passed away atnine months of age. It is said that Beatrice Shanley's mourning cries over the loss of her children can still be heard throughout the hotel. Guests have witnessed a woman in period clothing and the strong smell of perfume. Some say they can actually feel the sadness.

In September of 1915, Dr. Walter Nelson Thayer, Jr., who lived nearby, was backing his car out of the alley that ran between his home and the hotel when his five-year-old son, Walter Nelson Thayer III, jumped onto the running board and then fell off. Without seeing him, Dr. Thayer backed up over him. The young boy did not die from the accident but suffered severe head injuries. Many who have been to The Shanley say there is the spirit of a young boy present that plays in the attic. They're not sure who he is but think he could possibly be the young boy who was run over by the car years back who wanted to visit and remain at the hotel. No one really knows for sure, but the young boy in the attic is affectionally referred to as Jonathan.

After the deaths of the Shanley children, Esther Faughman, Beatrice Shanley's sister, and her husband, John, moved into the hotel along with their two daughters. Unfortunately, Beatrice had lost her sister, Esther, in 1918 due to influenza.

The Shanley had a barber who lived at the hotel with his family. His name was Peter Greger. One day, his youngest daughter, Rosie, was wandering around the nearby

Hoornbeek Farm which was located alongside The Shanley. She curiously lifted a wooden slab that she saw on the ground that covered a well. She lost her balance, hitting her head on the rocks as she fell. Her body was found two hours later. Devasted, the Greger family left the hotel and returned to Brooklyn. Many claim to see an apparition of a little girl they believe to be Rosie, who speaks to them in the hallways.

It was the Greger's apartment that later became an active bordello for those who frequented the Speakeasy and Gentlemen's Club.

On February 26, 1932, a raid was conducted on The Shanley, and that resulted in James Shanley and liquor bootlegger, John Powers, getting arrested. Having friends in high places, they were pardoned by the Roosevelts and set free. Some say they feel the presence of John Powers still lingering through the halls of the hotel.

When James Shanley passed away in 1937, Beatrice sold the hotel to Allen Hazen, who continued to run it until his death in 1971.

It is said that Allen liked his booze and would often need to sleep it off in his room at The Shanley before heading home to his wife. His room became known as the Silent Room, because whenever he would be up there sleeping, the staff and guests would all tiptoe around and be as quiet as possible so as to not wake him.

Ownership changes, once again, were made over the next two decades during which The Shanley Hotel became a tavern and named the James Shanley Tap Room. In 1991, it officially closed and was abandoned until 2005 when it was purchased by Salvatore Nicosia. Sal put his heart and soul into The Shanley until his death in July 2016.

In 2018, the hotel came under new management and was saved from being condemned.

Napanoch Man Dies on Tuesday

James Shanley, proprietor of Shanley's Hotel in Napanoch, died on Tuesday in the Benedictine Hospital, aged 61 years. Besides his wife, he is survived by two brothers, Patrick Shanley of Long Beach, L. I., and Peter Shanley of New York city; a sister, Mrs. John Burbege of Ireland, and two nieces, Marie and Katherine Saughnan. Mr. Shanley was brought to the hospital last Thursday suffering from heart trouble.

Mr. Shanley was a member of a well known restaurant family in New York city, and about 20 years ago opened the hotel at Napanoch. He was widely and favorably known throughout Ulster county. Friends will call at the late home in Napanoch on Thursday evening to recite the Rosary, and funeral services will be held from the home Friday morning at 10 o'clock and thence to St. Mary's Church in Ellenville, where services will be held at 10.30 o'clock with burial in the Fantinekill cemetery. Father Nilan, pastor of the church, will officiate. The bearers will be DeVere Smith, John Hoffman, Frank Hurd, John Gosselin, L. E. Westbrook, and Winnie Hoornbeek.

Mayor Met with New York Brokers

Mayor C. J. Heiselman while in New York city on Tuesday met with two of the largest real estate brokers in connection with prospects for factory sites. The mayor is using every effort to locate new industries in Kingston, and all prospects are closely followed up. Whenever it is learned that a large manufacturing plant is considering a change every effort is being used to induce that concern to consider Kingston as a likely site for the industry.

The national capitol has a single corridor 750 feet long running under both the Senate and House chambers.

Above left: Visitors leaving rocks on the well where little Rosie lost her life.

Above right: The obituary of James Shanley. [*The Kingston Daily Freeman, Wed, August 25, 1937*]

Above left: The Silent Room

Above right: The Silent room where Mr. Allen Hazen would go to sleep after he had one too many drinks.

When you pull up to the Shanley Hotel, you instantly feel transported back in time, and you can almost feel the history of the hotel just by looking at it. When you enter, you'll see a staircase facing you in a small hallway filled with old Victorian decor and charm. To the right is the gift shop and to the left is the Great Room. The Great Room is the main living room and meetup room for guests. Coffee is served here as well as snacks. Surrounding the fireplace are history books and composition notebooks that document experiences had by guests in each bedroom of the Shanley. There are photos on the table of Irish Mafia, which was very prominent in that area at one time.

The Séance Room was set up for mediums who visit the hotel and hold events there. There is also a dining room and kitchen area. There are a few stadium-style chairs there that date back to the 1850s. There is a mock speakeasy in the corner. The skeletal bartender "Winston" has a REM pod in his chest, but it never goes off when people are in the room and prefers to always go off once they leave. In the séance area, you'll find an authentic Victorian mourning gown. It is strongly felt that someone is attached to it, but it is unknown who. The couch is covered with haunted dolls and the Shanley now has up to 250 haunted dolls in its collection that have been brought in by people over the years. People bring them to the Shanley because they don't want them in their homes. The dolls that are seated on the couch all have names: Cal, Harold, Ian, Wilson, Archibald, and Debbie.

The whole area, at one time, was the kitchen and dining area, but it was redone after it wasn't salvageable. The floors are original.

The original old telephone booth still stands. Beatrice Shanley would hang around the facility every day in case the phone rang. It is said that she still waits

Above: Stained glass sign above the front door that says, "The Spirits Are Inn."

Below left: The foyer of The Shanley.

Below right: The Great Room

Above left: The Séance Room

Above right: The speakeasy area is complete with resident skeletal bartender "Winston" along with paranormal investigative items that are used as trigger objects during paranormal investigations conducted at The Shanley.

for calls. Next to the phone booth is the secret 8 x 8 little room in the floor where they hid the bootlegged liquor when it was a speakeasy.

In the back, you will find the old gentlemen's quarters. The room sleeps five comfortably but can sleep ten people with two to each bed. Plenty of drinking, gambling, and smoking took place in this room. There used to be a bowling alley in the back, but it no longer stands. Only men were allowed in here back in the day, and gambling in that room was done by men only. During paranormal investigations, a Spirit box will be used to interact with the spirits in the gentleman's quarters. Since gambling took place in that room, the staff would pick a card and ask the spirits (via the spirit box) what card was pulled. The spirit box will respond with the actual card. If the spirits win, the money goes into a box and is saved up to get the spirits the items they request during paranormal investigations and spirit box sessions.

The owners and staff of the Shanley have found that during many of the paranormal investigations and sessions held, there would be numerous spirits that are looking for a place to stay. Even after all these years, the hotel seems to be the place to stay in the spirit world.

One particular room of interest is the Scrying Room. This tiny room has (what is referred to as) a haunted mirror. When guests sit in front of the mirror and take photos, the mirror shows various strange images in the photos. Some of the images reportedly seen have been of bald-headed aliens, eyes that turn red and black, and faces that morph into other people. Usually after about ten to fifteen minutes, the images seem to manifest and can be captured in the photographs.

Above left: The original phone booth inside The Shanley. It is said that Beatrice Shanley still remains near this area waiting for calls.

Above right: Door to the storage area where liquor would be hidden and stored when they ran the speakeasy.

Above left: The Gentlemen's Room where the men would gather to drink, smoke, and play cards.

Above right: Scrying mirror

The bordello area is upstairs, and its two ladies of the evening, Maddie and Ann, are said to still haunt the area. The spirit of little Rosie, who is three years old, is also there as well. The spirit of Frank the bouncer is always felt as a steady presence.

Little Rosie loves books and dolls. Everyone who comes to her room reads her a bedtime story. All the spirits are still present and don't want to leave. Frank's suit hangs in the room. He was approximately 6'6" with dark hair and very handsome. The previous owners, Sal and his wife, had personally stenciled the floors by hand. They also did all the wallpapering.

The smell of cigarettes and cigars is a regular occurrence throughout the hotel.

The Roosevelt Suite was named after Eleanor Roosevelt, who would sleep in this room whenever she visited her best friend, Beatrice Shanley. In this room, a man named Vinny took his own life and hung himself in the 1920 stock market crash. There are reports of heavy pacing and furniture moving around, heard in the rooms below. People who slept in the bed in the actual room never hear the furniture moving but others downstairs do.

Rose's Room is the only room with a private bathroom. A child-sized spirit has been seen standing in the doorway of the bathroom. A large black entity has been seen that walks through the door, floats across the room, and stands and stares at whoever is in the bed. People who stay in this room have heard men arguing coming from the other side of the wall (which is a staff member's room). Back in the day, there were two mafia brothers who occupied the room and were fighting over the bed. One day, one of the brothers saw the other one walking up the sidewalk and he shot at him. He missed and the other brother shot back. There is

Above left: Rosie's Room

Above right: Anna's Room

Maddie's Room

Above left: Frank's suit hanging in the bordello

Above right: Toys for little Rosie and a pink dress in Rosie's Room

Above left: Bordello Staircase

Above right: The Roosevelt Room where a man hung himself after the 1920 stock market crash. People underneath that room can sometimes hear the sound of furniture shuffling and moving above them when no one is there.

actually a bullet hole through the window frame that goes to the top of the door in the staff member's room.

The Silent Room is named for the room Mr. Allen Hazen would stay in. Allen Hazen purchased the hotel from Beatrice Shanley in the 1940s. In the room is a photograph of him and his granddaughter sitting on the porch. When he was drinking, his wife wouldn't let him go home, so he would come to the Shanley to sleep it off. On those days, the staff would constantly say, "Shhh," because Mr. Hazen was asleep, and no one wanted to wake him. The smell of booze can be smelled on occasion. Some people sleep well in this room, and others don't sleep well at all.

Margurite's Room has a darker entity that tends to push people. She tends to demand respect and likes being asked permission to stay in her room. People knock before entering to be respectful. One of the staff members has a photo that shows a shadow figure of a male standing over her. A child-sized anomaly has also been seen standing alongside the bed. Impressions left by a ghost cat have been seen on the bed. A staff member also felt a hand going down her back along with a huge mist. Women and children's voices have been heard in the laundry room, but nobody was there.

Esther's Room was named for Beatrice's sister, Esther. In that room is a photo of her and her husband sitting on the sun porch. Esther passed in 1918 during the Spanish flu pandemic. At that time, she was eight months pregnant with a baby girl. They tried to save and revive the baby, but she passed away and was buried in her mother's arms.

Hanging in Esther's Room is a dress for Helen. Helen was only nine years old when she was murdered by the local butcher man's son. Helen Rosetta Glenn was the daughter of the Methodist minister in town. While her parents were attending a conference and were away for the day, a neighbor was left to care for the children. On June 26, 1935, Helen was walking to school to attend commencement exercises. On her way, she stopped at the local IGA store which sold meats, fruits, and candy, and was owned by Alfred Volckmann, Sr. Helen never returned home, and a massive search was conducted. Her body was later found near Basic Creek on Red Mill Road. According to the coroner, she had been raped and violently stabbed with a seven-inch blade. Since the IGA store was the last time anyone saw Helen alive, the police questioned Alfred Jr., who was nineteen years old and worked at the store. After being grilled by the police, he confessed to the murder, describing to the police how Helen came to his store and bought candy. He said he closed the store and took her to his bedroom and bound her to the bed. He went on to describe how he raped and beat her. When he was finished, he carried her unconscious body to Basic Creek where he drove a knife into her, killing her. Upset over what he had done, Alfred tried to commit suicide by drinking a bottle of iodine and a bottle of Lysol. The attempt was unsuccessful, and he was hospitalized for treatment. On May 27, 1936, Alfred

Above left: The Rose Room

Above right: The Silent Room

Above left: Marguerite's room is said to have a darker energy connected to it. People have often been pushed and shoved in this room.

Above right: Marguerite's Room

Above left: Esther's Room

Above right: A photo of Beatrice Shanley's sister, Esther, and her husband sitting on the front porch. Esther passed away in 1918 during the Spanish Flu epidemic.

GIRL, 9, ATTACKED AND SLAIN

The body of 9-year-old Helen Glenn (left) was found in a swamp near Greenville, N. Y., after the child, daughter of a Greenville minister, had been missing since Wednesday. She had been assaulted and stabbed. Photo shows the Glenn family, the Rev. Ernest Glenn, Mrs. Glenn, and Donald, Betty Ruth, and Ernest (right). (Associated Press Photo).

KILLER OF LITTLE GIRL CHARGED WITH MURDER

"Thrill" Slayer Taken From Hospital for Hearing; Used Lollypop as Lure

Greenville, N. Y. (AP).—Alfred E. Volckmann, confessed "thrill" slayer of 9 year old Helen Glenn, was arraigned on a charge of first degree murder shortly after dawn today and held for the grand jury.

Volckmann was taken from the Memorial Hospital at Catskill and whisked 15 miles to this village for the proceeding, which took less than ten minutes. Volckmann had been in the hospital since Saturday recovering from the effects of poison taken, he told State Police, after he attacked and stabbed little Helen on Thursday.

Volckmann, in his "full and detailed confession of the crime," said he lured the minister's daughter into his father's butcher shop with a lollypop, tied her to a bed in living quarters above and mistreated her.

When she fainted, the confession went on, the violin playing young man placed her unconscious form in his automobile and drove to a secluded spot on Basic Creek.

There he plunged a knife almost through her body, pounding it with his hand.

Members of New York state's "Scotland Yard" drew a confession from Alfred Volckmann, 19 (above) that he assaulted and killed nine-year-old Helen Glenn, daughter of a Greenville, N. Y. minister. Volckmann, a butcher boy, was the child's neighbor. (Associated Press Photo)

RENOVO HOTEL SOLD

BODY OF MISSING HELEN GLENN FOUND

Greenville, N. Y., Girl, 9, Had Been Stabbed to Death and Attacked.

MURDERER SOUGHT

GREENVILLE, N. Y., June 28 (AP). —The body of Greenville's "perfect school girl"—nine year old Helen Glenn—was found today in a nearby marsh, where it had been thrown after a vicious attack and murder.

It was found by two of the hundreds of townspeople who had hunted the child since she disappeared Wednesday night, and was turned over to Coroner M. E. Atkinson, who confirmed tonight the worst fears of the child's father, Rev. Ernest Glenn.

"Somebody near Greenville is suspected of attacking and killing my child," he told the Associated Press late today. Subdued excitement prevaded the town. Few residents ventured into the streets, and troopers in civilian clothes sat in tense circles in a downtown store.

Coroner Atkinson's verdict given at Catskill was that the child came to her death from a stab wound through the aorta, a main body blood vessel, and the liver. The single thrust caused death by internal hemorrhage. Dr. Atkinson said the child was perversely attacked.

On Way To School.

The brown haired child was last seen proudly en route to commencement exercises at grammar school, where she had earned the distinction of winning a prize for perfect attendance during the winter term.

Nothing more was seen of her until today. Under the impression the child was staying with friends, Mrs. Glenn did not report the absence of her daughter to police until yesterday morning. Their search fruitless, the police called in the state Scotland Yard, and welcomed townspeople in the hunt.

This morning hundreds of men, including former service men and Boy Scouts were afoot. Just after noon two of the searchers—John Zivelli and Roy Lawyer—spied a rough road near Basic creek and detached themselves from a party of troopers to investigate. At the end of the lane, near a junk pile, they saw the child's body, her clothing torn almost off.

The men called troopers, who sent the body to Dr. Atkinson at Catskill. He performed an autopsy during the afternoon, and reported at 7.10 p. m.

"This is a horrible case," he said. "I have information indicating that a suspect is under surveillance, but I do not think anything definite will develop until late tonight or early tomorrow."

Mrs. Glenn received the news of her daughter's death calmly, but collapsed late today, and tonight a physician was called to the home. Her condition is serious.

Above left: An article written about Helen Glenn in 1935 that was published in The Express. [*The Express 7-02-1935*]

Above right: Helen Glenn article published in The Rutland Daily Herald. [*The Rutland Daily Herald 6-29-1935 page 1*]

was found guilty and convicted of first-degree murder. On February 11, 1937, he was executed by electrocution at Sing Sing Prison.

The Shanley Hotel in Napanoch, New York, is notorious for being one of the most haunted places in America, with many unexplained occurrences attributed to the spirits of those who passed on. Claims over the years include laughing, crying, the sound of chimes, whistling, cold spots, piano music, the smell of cigars and cigarettes, cooking aromas, shadows, apparitions, spirits appearing in photographs, mists, disembodied voices, people being touched and pushed, feelings of being watched, as well as footsteps heard throughout the hotel.

The hotel's history is well documented on their website, and they even created a timeline of events to help readers follow the changes over the years. To provide an easier understanding and quick at-a-glance breakdown of all that has happened over the years, I am including that same timeline here:

Listed below is The Haunted Shanley Hotel Timeline (as seen on their website, TheHauntedShanleyHotel.com).

1845 - Thomas Ritch built a new hotel called Ritch's Hotel, but later renamed it as the Mansion House.

1851 - The hotel's name is changed to Hungerford's Hotel, after being bought by F. G. Hungerford.

1858 - In April, Hungerford sells the hotel to John Tonkin.

1866 - John Tonkin sells the hotel to A. J. Wood and it becomes the Topatcoke House.

1871 - In May, Wood sells the hotel to Aaron Schoonmaker, and it becomes the Napanoch Hotel.

1872 - Schoonmaker sells to Eli Dewitt Terwiliger.

1876 - October 31, James Louis Shanley is born.

1877 - Terwiliger sells the hotel to Civil War veterans, William Easman and his two brothers, Charles and Peter.

1884 - The Easman brothers sell to Frederick B. Bridgens.

1887 - Adolf Wagner purchases the hotel.

1895 - March 18, the hotel burns down to its foundation, after a nearby house catches fire and spreads.

1895 - By September a new building frame is erected.

1895 - In November the hotel reopens for business as the Colonial Hotel.

1898 - Wagner sells to Mary Roos and they change the name of the hotel back to the Hotel Napanoch.

1900 – U.S. Federal Census shows George Gosselin as the owner.

1902 - Allen H. Hazen is born.

1906 - James Louis Shanley purchases the Colonial Hotel for $10,000.

1907 - Charles Byrnes fell from a window, but survived.

1908 - A new addition is built for the hotel, including a bowling alley, barbershop, billiard room, and second-floor apartments.

1910 - A barbershop opens with a barber named Peter Greger from Brooklyn, NY.

1910 - April 26, James and Beatrice are married in the hotel.

1911 - July 18, Kathleen Shanley is born to James and Beatrice.

1911 - On May 26, the barber's daughter, Jeanette Roseanne "Rosie" Greger, drowns in the well of the Hoornbeek Farm across the street from the hotel.

1912 - On January 6, Kathleen Shanley dies at the age of five months and twenty-four days.

1913 - On September 10 James Shanley Jr. is born. The hotel's name would soon be changed to Shanley's Hotel.

1914 - On January 21 James Shanley Jr. dies at the age of four months and eleven days old.

1915 - Dr. Walter Nelson Thayer, Jr. accidentally runs over his five-year-old son, Walter Nelson Thayer III, after the boy climbed onto the running board as the car was backing out of the alley between the hotel and the doctor's home. The boy sustained severe head injuries but did not die from the accident.

1916 - January 30 William Shanley is born to James and Beatrice.

1916 - In February, there is a fire in the ice house, and a new auto fire truck is credited with saving the hotel from destruction.

1916 - On November 9, William Shanley dies at the age of nine months and ten days old.

1920s - The hotel operates as a speakeasy with bootleg liquor hidden away in a secret basement room under the bar.

1932 - The hotel is raided for booze during the Prohibition Era.

1933 - James and Beatrice attend the Inaugural Ball at Washington, D.C.

1933 - On August 3, future first lady, Eleanor Roosevelt, is a guest at the hotel.

1937 - August 26, James Louis Shanley dies.

1941 - April 13, there is a fire at the hotel due to a faulty chimney.

1944 - Beatrice sells the hotel to Allen H. Hazen

1961 - November 27, Beatrice Shanley dies.

1967 - Nelson F. Waters purchases the hotel from Al.

1971 - August 26, Allen H. Hazen dies.

1973 - G. Edward Trumbull purchases the hotel.

1991 - The hotel closes down.

2005 - Salvatore Nicosia purchases the hotel and discovers it is home to several spirits.

2007 - The Shanley Hotel is reopened.

2016 - July 5, Salvatore Nicosia passes away.

2017 - In December, the hotel was condemned and closed after a time of mixed reviews and poor management.

2018 - The hotel is reopened under new management.

The Shanley Hotel is well known for its history and paranormal activity and has been featured in many of the paranormal TV shows over the years. The hotel offers a unique blend of hospitality and mystery. Their website lists a detailed history and timeline of the hotel.

In 2018, the hotel was purchased by new owners and all new management whose kind hospitality makes it a wonderful place for all who come to visit and for all those who remain. Tours and booking information are listed on their website. The owners and staff of the hotel are happy to accommodate their guests. Whether it's for a visit to tour the hotel, schedule a paranormal investigation, or book a stay, it does not disappoint!

Hallway

24

The Witch of Esperance, Cobleskill, New York

The town of Esperance is located near Cobleskill, New York. During the Revolution, its name was State Bridge. It's a small village that carries a sad story from the 1800s. General William North was an aid of George Washington and purchased the land and his daughter, Henrietta, changed the name from State Bridge to Esperance.

During the Napoleonic wars, a French soldier, along with his wife and children, were looking for a home while wandering towards the west. They found a home they loved in Esperance and decided to stay. Unfortunately, the man died, leaving his wife and children to fend for themselves. The wife could not speak English, which made it difficult for her to communicate and make friends in the town. She isolated herself and kept busy tending to her chickens and her garden. The townspeople found her to be an odd woman and didn't really know what to make of her. They nicknamed her "the Grenadier Woman" and because she was so different and strange, they all began to think of her as a witch.

The French widow began being blamed for failing crops as well as for sick and dying cattle. They accused her of using her apron to cross Schoharie Creek, and then put it back on when she reached the other side, completely dry. As ridiculous as it seems, the villagers blamed every single bad occurrence on the widow.

The townspeople took matters into their own hands and met in a nearby Presbyterian church to take a vote as to what to do with the woman. Unfortunately, the vote was that she be put to death. With that said, men were chosen to carry out the task. They prepared a batch of silver bullets and went to her home. They peered through her cabin window and found her cooking on an open fire. There were two children who were on the floor playing beside her while she cooked. The men took the opportunity to fire their guns, killing her.

The woman was buried with a stake through her head, and they planted an evergreen tree over her so the roots could hold her down and prevent her from seeking vengeance.

The story wasn't clear about who the two children were that were playing near her at the time of her death. One would assume they were her own children, but that was never documented. It is said that one of the boys who witnessed the

An old photo published in 1912 of the home of the Witch of Esperance. [*The Cambridge Sentinel, She Died For Witchcraft, Volume IX Number 49, 21 September 1912*]

occurrence lived to be in his nineties and was appointed postmaster by Andrew Jackson and then removed by Grover Cleveland in 1885.

There's another version of the story that's slightly different. In this version, a headstone was found on the property next to the old Kniskern home on top of a foothill. The headstone read "Elizabeth Kniskern, wife of John, died in 1854".

Legend has it that in this version, Elizabeth was left to run the farm after her husband die. She had only one child. In this version of the story, her son was being persuaded to enlist in the army by the town postmaster, who also acted as a recruitment officer. Elizabeth, being furious by this, warned the postmaster not to sign her son up or she would put a hex on the town. Unfortunately, the son signed up and died during his service. Elizabeth said she was going to hex the town and shortly after, strange things began to happen. Barns burned down, the post office caught on fire, and animals began to get sick and die. It was at that point that the townspeople felt she was a true witch and they voted on her death. The men chosen went to her home and shot her with a silver bullet. They buried her upside down underneath an evergreen tree which supposedly still stands to this day.

The two stories are very similar, and they both have the same unfortunate ending. Was she really a witch like the legend says, or was she just an innocent woman who was accused of witchcraft and killed for the sole fact that she was different from everyone else?

The New York Folklore Society and the William G. Pomeroy Foundation erected a folklore marker dedicated to the Witch of Esperance.

The Marker reads:

Esperance Witch
Lived Near Here In 1800s.
French Settler Accused Of
Witchcraft By New England
Settlers. Killed By Silver
Bullet Shot Through Her Window

Thankfully the days of witch hunters are long behind us.

25

The Witch of Nyack, Nyack, New York

Not all the witch trials were held in Salem, Massachusetts. There was an old legend that took place in the year 1815, about a woman Jane "Naut" Kanniff, who lived in Clarksville and was often referred to as the "Witch of West Nyack." According to Green's 1886 book, *The History of Rockland County*, Jane Kanniff, a twice-married widow, became the target of witchcraft accusations.

Jane was a very eccentric woman who was known to have odd habits. She wore her hair strangely and wore mismatched clothing of assorted colors. Because of her odd behavior and appearance, many thought she could be insane. She was a very independent woman who lived alone in a run-down, dilapidated old house in West Nyack. She kept to herself and hardly ever socialized with anyone. Her home was usually coated in crows which only fueled the townsfolk into believing she was a witch, since crows were usually associated with witchcraft during that time period. She was the widow of a Scottish physician and a single mother with a young boy named Tobias Lowrie from a previous marriage. Jane had learned a lot from her physician husband and would often make medicines and tinctures that she learned how to make using her husband's pharmacology book.

It was unheard during that time period for a woman to practice any form of medicine, and if she did, then she was a witch. Despite her weirdness, she was a kind woman who offered remedies to those who were ill and went to her for help. She used her skills to help the sick.

Legend says that a landowner threatened to seize her property and wanted it for his own. Jane refused to allow this to happen. The story goes on to say that the landowner woke the next morning to find all his crops wilted and dying. The townspeople felt that Jane did this with her magical abilities.

Children would run past her house for fear of getting caught and having a spell put upon them. The local housewives were finding themselves having difficulty churning butter. Several of them claimed to have discovered a horseshoe burned into the bottom of their churns upon emptying them, fearing the devil ruined their butter. One member of the town found the town's best milking cow just standing in a farm wagon and after that was found to have yielded no milk. The townspeople didn't think of other potential causes for these occurrences. Their immediate thought went directly to Naut Kanniff being responsible because she was a witch.

The townspeople decided it was time to put her on trial for witchcraft. The town's resident physician was the people's choice for judge. The jury was composed of farmers from the neighborhood. The site chosen for the trial was the De Clark-Polhemus Mill at the center of the hamlet just south of Pye's Corner. The mode of trial was by balance. They felt that if a woman was a witch, she would weigh less than the bible. Polhemus Mill was the only location available that had scales that large to accommodate the test. The Dutch bible that was used was huge and made out of wood and brass. Naut Kanniff was brought to the mill, was seated in one dish of the big mill scale, and the bible on the other. If the bible outweighed Naut Kanniff and lowered, it would be conclusive evidence that she was a witch. If to the contrary, she raised the bible, it was equally conclusive that she was innocent. When they pulled the pin from the scales, Naut Kanniff outweighed the bible, declaring her innocence and not a witch.

The witch trial of Jane Naut Kanniff of 1816 has been noted as being the last witch trial in the state of New York. Approximately 50,000 innocent women were killed for witchcraft in Europe and America Between the fifteenth and eighteenth centuries. The story of Jane Kanniff will continue on as an integral part of American folklore and will always be known as the last witch trial in the state of New York.

The De Clark-Polhemus Mill [NY Heritage Digital Collection]

Bibliography

1039thebreezealbany.com/ghost-hunters-communicate-with-female-spirit-in-upstate-ny-haunted-home/

agoda.com/tarrytown-house-estate-on-the-hudson_2/hotel/irvington-ny-us.
    html?ds=EKguM1f64BhyMa7S

backpackerverse.com/dead-girl-causes-nightmares-at-the-bulls-head-inn/

Bacon, E. M., *Chronicles Of Tarrytown And Sleepy Hollow - Illustrated Fourth Impression* (Gp
    Putnam's Sons, New York And London, The Knickerbocker Press 1902)

bannermancastle.org/history/

Barber, J. W., Howe, H., *Historical Collections of the State of New York*, (Chatham Square, S. Tuttle 1832)

barryvilleny.com/members/burn-brae-mansion/

bearfortparanormal.com/the-italian-villa-restaurant-of-warwick-ny-the-roy-vail-house/

Bertangue Green, M.D, F., *The History of Rockland County, reprint of the original 1886 edition*,
    (New City, N.Y., The Historical Society of Rockland Co.1986)

burnbraemansion.com/history.htm

clements.umich.edu/exhibit/spy-letters-of-the-american-revolution/stories-of-spies/death-of-john-andre/

ctinsider.com/living/article/CT-Leatherman-urban-legend-17517012.php

daily.jstor.org/the-legend-of-the-leatherman/

dailyfreeman.com/2012/10/28/napanoch-boasts-haunting-inn-with-shanley-hotel-video/

dailymail.co.uk/news/article-2666837/Inside-home-Supreme-Court-Justices-serial-killers-The-
    haunting-images-abandoned-New-York-prison-youth-offender-facility-historic-rehab-clinic.html

biography.com/crime-figure/joseph-sullivan

warwickvalleyliving.com/education/12-land-of-dreams,-imaginings,-and-visions-a-history-of-the-
    mid-orange-correctional-facility-site-from-the-indian-era-to-the-present

iarchives.nysed.gov/xtf/view?docId=ead/findingaids/W0033.xml;chunk.
    id=fullfalink;brand=default

nytimes.com/1984/08/26/nyregion/medical-center-where-inmates-with-aids-are-treated.html

facebook.com/pg/whsny.org/about/?ref=page_internal

orangecountygov.com/1589/Deeds

hudsonvalleysojourner.com/sojourners-picks/alcohol-drug-treatment-hudson-valley/

wsj.com/articles/new-york-prison-escape-stirs-bad-memories-for-former-hostage-1434071577

correctionhistory.org/html/chronicl/docs2day/mid-orangecf.html

albertwisnerlibrary.org/Factsandhistory/History/MOCF/

dailymail.co.uk/news/article-2666837/Inside-home-Supreme-Court-Justices-serial-killers-The-
    haunting-images-abandoned-New-York-prison-youth-offender-facility-historic-rehab-clinic.html

dailyvoice.com/new-york/putnam/lifestyle/ghosts-and-all-smalley-inn-has-been-carmel-mainstay-for-
    over-century/687500/

digitalcollections.smu.edu/digital/collection/ryr/id/367

dutchess.org/history/bannerman_castle_history

dutchesstourism.com/listings/haunted-history-tour

dutchesstourism.com/listingsv/miss-fannys-victorian-party-house146Top of Form

einnews.com/pr_news/550422790/the-enslin-haunted-mansion-goes-on-real-estate-market-for-first-
    time-ever-in-upstate-new-york

facebook.com/136488103065534/posts/silvios-was-featured-as-the-haunted-villa-when-john-zaffis-
    and-the-team-from-syf/3385325901515055/

facebook.com/burnbraemansion/

Friends of the Old Dutch Burial Ground, *The Junior League of Westchester-On-Hudson, Inc, Tales of the Old Dutch Burial Ground* (Schenectady, New York, Benchemark Printing Inc., 2012)

guides.rcls.org/c.php?g=128582&p=840328

hauntedhistorytrail.com/

Headly, Russel, *The History of Orange County, New York* (Van Deusen and Elms, Middletown, NY, 1908)

hellowarwickvalley.com/aview/silvios-7886a-49nw2

Historical and Genealogical Record Dutchess and Putnam Counties New York (Poughkeepsie, NY, Press of The A. V. Haight Co., 1912)

history.com/news/7-bizarre-witch-trial-tests

history.nycourts.gov/wp-content/uploads/2019/07/County-Legal-History_Westchester-compressed.pdf

hmdb.org

hudsonriver.com

hvmag.com

i95rock.com/tarrytown-chinese-eatery-named-among-americas-creepiest-haunted-restaurants/

iloveny.com/blog/post/stay-at-new-yorks-haunted-hotels-and-inns-if-you-dare/

intelligence.gov/evolution-of-espionage/revolutionary-war/british-espionage/john-andre

Lathrop, E., *Historic Houses of Early America* (New York, NY, Robert M. McBride and Co, 1927)

law.cornell.edu/wex/stambovsky_v._ackley#:~:text=The%20Court%20held%20that%2C%20whether,as%20a%20matter%20of%20law

Lindsay, John S., *The Mormons & The Theater,* (Salt Lake City Utah, Shepard Book Co, 1905)

loc.gov/item/93510375/

McDonald, G., "Return to Bannerman's," *North South Trader Magazine*, Vol IV, pp. 24-31 (March April 1977)

metropolismag.com/projects/tarrytown-estates-renovation/

midatlanticdaytrips.com

minisink.org/laurelgrove.html

missfannys.com/

mountvernon.org/library/digitalhistory/digital-encyclopedia/article/john-andre/

news.hamlethub.com/carmel/neighbors/2898-tarrytown-restaurant-goosefeathers-named-one-of-the-17-creepiest-haunted-bars-and-restaurants-in-america

newyorkalmanack.com/2014/06/the-architectural-legacy-of-george-ross-mackenzie/

newyorkalmanack.com/categories/history/

newyorkhauntedhouses.com

newyorkupstate.com/homes/2021/09/must-see-upstate-ny-home-haunted-house-comes-with-ghostly-roommates-spooky-charm.html

npr.org/2011/05/26/136649653/leatherman-remains-a-mystery-even-in-death

nymetroparents.com/article/haunted-history-trail-in-the-hudson-valley-ny

nytimes.com/1872/02/17/archives/the-extreme-penalty-buckhout-the-sleepy-hollow-murderer-at-last.html

oddthingsiveseen.com/2012/10/sleepy-hollow-more-macabre-than-i-knew.html

oracle.newpaltz.edu/top-10-hudson-valley-haunted-places/

Owens, W., *Pocantico Hills 1609-1959, Sleepy Hollow Restorations 1960* (Tarrytown, New York Library of Congress)

patch.com/new-york/tarrytown/a-new-year-s-brutal-triple-murder-in-1870

patch.com/new-york/tarrytown/where-the-ghosts-are

patch.com/new-york/whiteplains/an-aggregated-account-of-buckout-road-urban-legends

Pleska, E., *The Horrific Story of Buckout Road* (Right On Dudes Productions, 2021)

puzzleboxhorror.com/the-horrifying-legend-of-buckout-road/

q1057.com/the-famous-haunts-of-tarrytown-ny-have-you-heard-of-spook-rock/

recordonline.com/story/news/local/port-jervis/2014/12/19/ghost-detective-found-unusual-activity/35703967007/

recordonline.com/story/news/local/port-jervis/2014/12/19/ghost-detective-found-unusual-activity/35703967007/

recordonline.com/story/news/local/port-jervis/2020/10/29/weird-sightings-materialize-in-port-jervis-history/114539906/

recordonline.com/story/news/local/port-jervis/2020/10/29/weird-sightings-materialize-in-port-jervis-history/114539906/

rightondudes.com/buckoutroad.html
riverjournalonline.com/news/remembering-a-music-hall-visionary/750/
roadtrippers.com/magazine/haunted-shanley-hotel-new-york/
rocklandtimes.com/2022/10/31/hoehm-town-happeningsthe-story-of-jane-naut-kanniff-the-witch-of-west-nyack/
Ruttenber, E.M., Clark, L. H., *History of Orange County New York*, (Philadelphia, Everts & Pece, 1881)
scaredandalone.com/whats-haunting-burn-brae-mansion/
scenicwilddelawareriver.com/entries/laurel-grove-cemetery-port-jervis-ny/ac5476e5-f5ce-4abf-b94b-f91dd572e98b
scenicwilddelawareriver.com/entries/laurel-grove-cemetery-port-jervis-ny/ac5476e5-f5ce-4abf-b94b-f91dd572e98b
SilviosItalianVilla.com
sleepyhollowcountry.com
suzannespellen.substack.com/p/bannerman-island-and-the-improbable
Talman, W. B., *How Things Began … in Rockland County and Places Nearby* (New City, N.Y., The Historical Society of Rockland County, 1977)
tarrytownhouseestate.com
tarrytownny.gov/parks-and-recreation-department
The Historical Company, *Prominent Families of New York*, (New York, Nicoll and Roy Co, 1898)
The Historical Society, *Images of America, Tarrytown and Sleepy Hollow* (Charleston, South Carolina, Arcadia Publishing 1997)
timesunion.com/hudsonvalley/outdoors/article/aliens-in-the-Hudson-Valley-ufo-museum-opens-16147894.php
timesunion.com/news/article/For-sale-in-Troy-a-house-where-there-are-bumps-16450629.php
Tompkins, Arthur S., *Historical Record to the Close of the Nineteenth Century of Rockland County* (New York, ed. Legare Press Nyack, N.Y., 1902)
tumblr.com/rocklandhistoryblog/100465214040/jane-naut-kanniff-the-witch-of-west-nyack-by
tumblr.com/rocklandhistoryblog/100465214040/jane-naut-kanniff-the-witch-of-west-nyack-by
usghostadventures.com/haunted-cities/savannahs-most-haunted/laurel-grove-cemetery/
visitwestchesterny.com/listing/tarrytown-house-estate/535/
wandercuse.com/spend-a-night-at-burn-brae-mansion-one-of-nys-most-haunted-hotels/
warwickadvertiser.com/news/local-news/silvios-italian-villa-opens-new-outdoor-patio-CQWA20120626120629965
warwickadvertiser.com/news/local-news/silvios-italian-villa-opens-new-outdoor-patio-CQWA20120626120629965
warwickvalleyliving.com/education/12-land-of-dreams,-imaginings,-and-visions-a-history-of-the-mid-orange-correctional-facility-site-from-the-indian-era-to-the-present
iarchives.nysed.gov/xtf/view?docId=ead/findingaids/W0033.xml;chunk.id=fullfalink;brand=default
washingtonpost.com/lifestyle/travel/in-the-hudson-valley-two-grand-mansions-make-one-great-hotel/2011/01/13/ABx2JkD_story.html
westchesterarchives.com/ht/muni/tarrytn/andre.htm
westchestermagazine.com/life-style/haunted-westchester-locations/
westchesterwoman.org/buckout-road-white-plains-the-westchester-streets-haunted-history/
wgpfoundation.org/historic-markers/laurel-grove/
wgpfoundation.org/historic-markers/laurel-grove/
wikipedia.org/wiki/John_Andr%C3%A9
wikipedia.org/wiki/Julia_Dean_(actress,_born_1830)
wikipedia.org/wiki/Leatherman_(vagabond)
wikipedia.org/wiki/Pollepel_Island
wikipedia.org/wiki/Smalley%27s_Inn_%26_Restaurant
wpdh.com/buckout-road/
wpdh.com/most-haunted-hudson-valley-location-2-victorian-party-house/
wrrv.com/haunted-historical-hudson-valley-landmarks/
wrrv.com/hudson-valley-cemetery-added-to-haunted-history-trail/
youtube.com/watch?v=c-XH3bPines